# New

# New

*Understanding Our Need*
*for Novelty and Change*

WINIFRED GALLAGHER

THE PENGUIN PRESS
*New York*
*2012*

THE PENGUIN PRESS
Published by the Penguin Group
Penguin Group (USA) Inc., 375 Hudson Street, New York, New York 10014,
U.S.A. • Penguin Group (Canada), 90 Eglinton Avenue East, Suite 700, Toronto,
Ontario, Canada M4P 2Y3 (a division of Pearson Penguin Canada Inc.) •
Penguin Books Ltd, 80 Strand, London WC2R 0RL, England • Penguin Ireland,
25 St. Stephen's Green, Dublin 2, Ireland (a division of Penguin Books Ltd) •
Penguin Books Australia Ltd, 250 Camberwell Road, Camberwell, Victoria 3124,
Australia (a division of Pearson Australia Group Pty Ltd) • Penguin Books
India Pvt Ltd, 11 Community Centre, Panchsheel Park, New Delhi—110 017,
India • Penguin Group (NZ), 67 Apollo Drive, Rosedale, Auckland 0632,
New Zealand (a division of Pearson New Zealand Ltd) •
Penguin Books (South Africa) (Pty) Ltd, 24 Sturdee Avenue,
Rosebank, Johannesburg 2196, South Africa

Penguin Books Ltd, Registered Offices: 80 Strand, London WC2R 0RL, England

First published in 2011 by The Penguin Press,
a member of Penguin Group (USA) Inc.

Library of Congress Cataloging-in-Publication Data

Gallagher, Winifred.
New : understanding our need for novelty and change / Winifred Gallagher.
p.   cm.
Includes bibliographical references and index.
ISBN 978-1-59420-320-6
1. Change (Psychology)   2. New and old—Psychological aspects.
3. Risk-taking (Psychology)   I. Title.
BF637.C4G35 2012
158—dc23
2011029943

Printed in the United States of America
1   3   5   7   9   10   8   6   4   2

DESIGNED BY AMANDA DEWEY

ALWAYS LEARNING                                                    PEARSON

*The universe is change; our life is what our thoughts make it.*

—Marcus Aurelius, *Meditations*

# Contents

# PART III Neophilia Today

# New

## Introduction

# What's New?

SCIENTISTS, ARTISTS, AND SCHOLARS have cast us as analytical thinkers and passionate romantics, pragmatic toolmak-
ers and spiritual souls, aggressive competitors and cooperative
altruists. None of these views is complete, yet each has illumi-
nated human beings in a helpful way. Now our fast-paced world
invites us to see ourselves in yet another light—this time as
nature's *virtuosos* of change, who are biologically as well as psy-
chologically primed to engage with novelty.

Our genius for responding to the new and different distinguishes us from all other creatures, saved us from extinction 80,000 years ago, and has fueled our progress from the
long epoch of the hunter-gatherers through the agricultural
and industrial eras into the information age. Suddenly, however, we're confronting many, many more new objects and

subjects, from products to ideas to chunks of data, than have ever existed before, and they're coming at us faster and faster. We sometimes feel taxed if not overwhelmed, but *New* argues that our rewards will far outweigh our frustrations if we stay true to the evolutionary purpose of our neophilia, or affinity for novelty: to help us adapt to, learn about, or create the new things that matter, while dismissing the rest as distractions.

Novelty comes in countless forms, but to see how we're dealing with one especially timely manifestation, let's tap our brain's ability to travel through space and time—itself a triumph of neophilia—to visit a large airport just after mechanical trouble has delayed the 9:00 A.M. flight to Denver. The waiting area is immediately transformed into a satellite laboratory that's part of a vast, ongoing experiment with a new way of life based on information technology. Whatever their size or function, these machines can be defined in two words: novelty generators.

Charlotte, a high-school teacher, and her nine-year-old son, Jack, adjust quickly to the irksome change in plans. She takes out her laptop, scans the headlines on a news Web site, then settles down to fine-tune the presentation she's going to give at a professional conference. To limit distractions while she works, she sends her calls to voice mail and checks her e-mail just once an hour or so. The better to enjoy his holiday, Jack decides to get some homework out of the way and pulls out his new tablet computer, which is already almost a body part. First he goes over Spanish vocabulary for an upcoming test, then he does some research on the Oregon Trail. After working for a while, he takes a break to e-mail a few friends and cajoles his mom into playing a little chess, which he's learned from a special app.

When they finally board the plane three hours later, Charlotte is pleased that she managed to turn a setback into a productive morning and rewards herself by reading her e-book mystery. Jack shows a fascinated older passenger a computer game that he usually enjoys with the family's cat: with paw or finger, the players try to catch a fiendishly evasive glowing red "mouse." This mother and child are classic neophiles, who have a positive but well-balanced attitude toward novelty. They focus selectively on those new things—here, pieces of electronic information—that help them to learn or accomplish something worthwhile, including reasonable amounts of R&R, and smoothly adjust to and exploit change, such as the sudden hitch in their plans.

A young partner in an Internet start-up, Ted is first riled up by the unexpected change, alternating between punching excuses for missing a big meeting into his BlackBerry and phoning headquarters to bark orders at subordinates. Within moments, however, he's escorting a striking fellow passenger to an impromptu breakfast, complete with Bloody Marys. When more exciting options seem exhausted, he pops open his razor-thin laptop and, despite frequent checks for messages and the odd *Call of Duty* gaming break, comes up with an edgy marketing idea.

Ted excels at inventive thinking, corporate competition, and personal charm, but by the time his outraged seatmate chides him for texting as the plane taxis down the runway, his morning has produced mixed results. He experienced some *frisson* and did some good work, but he also generated *agita* for others and wasted time on distractions. This neophiliac, or extreme novelty-seeker, responds to change and the new as sources of the stimulation he craves, which helps explain both his talent for brainstorming and his powerful attraction to pretty strangers, cocktails, and alluring information machines.

Alan, an older accountant who expects things to go as planned, shifts between quietly fuming at the delayed flight and worrying about the mechanical *snafu* that caused it. To calm down, he retreats into his morning routine of reading the print versions of the *Wall Street Journal* and the *New York Times* and then reviews a big client's tax records for the second time. He's resigned to taking his cell phone on business trips but has no interest in other gadgets. His colleagues get annoyed when he resists learning a new software program or procedure, but like their customers, they also value his attention to detail and wariness of risk. When he takes his seat on the plane, this neophobe, who responds to the new and unexpected with caution or anxiety, has done his best to make this morning much like any other, which is his ideal.

Like most behavior, neophilia occurs on a spectrum. Ted and Alan are situated toward its high and low ends, while Charlotte and Jack represent the moderate majority, who are arrayed along the capacious middle range. Their different responses to novelty and change suggest the three basic ways in which individuals interpret life's great imperative: to survive and thrive by balancing the sometimes conflicting needs to avoid risk and approach rewards.

Vital information about potential threats and resources is likelier to come from things that are new or unfamiliar than from the same old same old. Because they can affect survival, nature ensures that all living creatures react to novelty and change. A swerving car on the highway, a jump in your bad cholesterol, or a drop in a stock's value rivets your attention and jangles your nerves, which prime you to protect yourself from harm. On the other hand, an exciting IPO, intriguing job offer, or innovative home design can also attract your focus, lure you into learning new things, and perhaps increase your well-being.

Dodging risks and seeking rewards both make good evolutionary sense, but variations in nature and nurture incline individuals to prioritize them differently. The approximately 10 percent to 15 percent of us who are neophobes like Alan are biased toward staying safe, and the roughly similar number of neophiliacs like Ted, toward seeking bonuses. The remaining 70 percent to 80 percent are moderate neophiles of different degrees who, like Charlotte and Jack, want to be neither scared stiff by too much novelty and change nor bored stiff by too little. They tend to seek the new and different more in their intellectual, creative, and recreational pursuits than in domains that require continuity and familiarity, such as their close relationships or professional commitments. In other words, they follow Alexander Pope's advice: "Be not the first by whom the new are tried, nor yet the last to lay the old aside."

It might not seem so at first glance, but neophilia's extremes are important to the success of the group as a whole. Nature promotes a species' survival and flexibility by ensuring diversity within a population, not an individual. Whatever the costs for a particular person, particularly at the continuum's high and low ends, the roughly 1–5–1 proportion of those who generally approach, weigh, or avoid new things is good for the commonweal. Adventurous neophiliacs like Ted may live too fast and die too young, but they also explore, experiment, and otherwise push the envelope for the rest of us in productive ways. Cautious neophobes can be stodgy worrywarts, but had there been more careful, risk-averse sorts like Alan in Wall Street's boardrooms, we might have avoided a major recession. Wherever we sit on the spectrum, however, we can learn to manage our responses to novelty and change more skillfully.

A word here about language: Since its emergence more than a century ago, *neophilia* has meant different things in different domains, including biology, social criticism, and information technology. (For more information, please see *Notes*.) This flexible term is used in these pages to avoid some notably confusing academic jargon and, more important, to suggest a fresh, more expansive perspective on our species' unique affinity for the new and different. We express this capacity in ways that overlap yet are partly distinct, including the transient emotions of curiosity and interest, enduring traits such as boldness, shyness, and so-called novelty seeking, and both the adventurous temperament and the creative personality. Lewis and Clark's voyage of discovery may differ from Stephen

Hawking's journeys into the unknown, yet both forms of exploration have important things in common, starting with their essential function: enhancing our survival and well-being by engaging with the new.

PART I OF *New* explores neophilia's origins and basic mind-body mechanics. We evolved in an African cradle of extraordinary environmental upheavals. Many species, as well as some human subspecies who were our close cousins, couldn't adjust to the cataclysmic changes and died out. However, *Homo sapiens* developed the capacity to figure out how to live in humid forests and dry deserts, flat plains and mountain ranges. These early ancestors also explored new mental realms. They learned to interpret the world in the symbolic terms of words, numbers, and pictures and to channel the uniquely human gift of self-awareness into neophilia's creative expressions, foremost of which is the personal universe that lies between our ears. The big "surprise detector" brains we inherited from them orient us to new developments in the world, help us filter out the insignificant ones, and supply the emotions that motivate us to approach, avoid, or consider those that could be important in one way or another.

Part II looks at the myriad ways in which individuals can express the general human capacity for neophilia, which is both a state, or transient psychobiological condition, and an abiding trait, or individual characteristic. Whether you're a bold Theodore Roosevelt or a reclusive Emily Dickinson, nothing reveals your personality more clearly and immediately than your reaction to new things over time and across many situations. A blind date, a hurricane, or a strange city arouses all of us. However, differences in our genes, neurochemistry, and brain structure, as well as life experience, incline us, like Charlotte, Ted, and Alan, to respond to that excitement differently.

Part III examines the profound ways in which our environments, both mental and physical, shape our attitudes to novelty and change. Like individuals, societies struggle to balance the need to survive, which prioritizes safety and stability, with the desire to thrive, which requires stimulation and exploration. For most of history, this tug-of-war has inclined cultural change, like the biological sort, to occur not in a smooth progression but in an uneven, unpredictable process of fits and starts that scientists call "punctuated equilibrium." Something new, whether climate change, an important tool such as the plow or computer, or a political upheaval, prompts a period of innovation that takes a society to the next level. Like the Pax Romana, this stable plateau can last for a great while until, perhaps following an era of decline like the Dark Ages, there's another leap forward, as in the Renaissance.

The vibrant Muslim world's inward turning in the thirteenth century, which has only recently begun to reverse, is a timely illustration of the way in which a society, particularly in risky times and places, can crouch into a conservative, defensive attitude toward the new and different that generates long spells of stasis and neophobia. Since the eighteenth century in the West, however, when the convergence of the Industrial Revolution's technology and the Enlightenment's ideas up-ended the historical pattern of fits-and-starts innovation, the amount of novelty and rate of change have increased at an ever-accelerating pace.

Biological as well as cultural influences can incline some populations to be more enthusiastic about the new than others. For example, the frequency of a certain gene that's linked to robust novelty seeking varies greatly around the globe. Its prevalence among Westerners of European descent is a hefty 25 percent, for example, yet it's very rare in traditionally conservative China.

At this point in our warp-speed information age, our well-being demands that we understand and control our neophilia lest it control us. We already crunch four times more data—e-mail, tweets, searches, music, video, and traditional media—than we did just thirty years ago, and this deluge shows no signs of slackening. To thrive amid unprecedented amounts of novelty, we must shift from being mere seekers of the new to being connoisseurs of it.

The digital revolution's tremendous benefits include access to nearly all the world's knowledge, greater efficiency, more freedom from boundaries such as home and office or artist and spectator, new ways to bond, and a riotous explosion of popular culture. In what might be a massive experiment designed by a fiendish psychologist, however, the combination of our innate interest in novelty and the huge increase in it can also generate a mental version of the perfect storm. Both as individuals and as a society, we can become so distracted by trivial yet instantly gratifying new things that we lose sight of neophilia's grand purpose of selectively focusing us on the important ones that help us to learn, create, and adapt to a changing world.

To understand and make proper use of our neophilia, we need to look beyond secondary issues, such as out-of-control consumerism, attention problems, and electronics addiction, to see it as a metaphenomenon that underlies much of our behavior. This big-picture perspective on our special affinity for novelty has long been missing from our conversation. *New* is an effort to start that discussion, sparked by provocative insights from neuroscientists, psychologists, anthropologists, psychiatrists, media theorists, marketers, and others who closely monitor the fast-changing culture's pulse.

The skillful management of our neophilia is essential if we're to turn the twenty-first century's challenges into opportunities. Our history shows that we have the potential to succeed in such an ambitious undertaking. After all, we had evolved the necessary neurological hardware for speech more than a millennium before we invented language. The first step is to understand ourselves as *Homo novus*—nature's scientists and artists of the new.

A WONDERFUL LITTLE STORY about five-year-old Albert Einstein, who was very slow to speak and whose parents feared he was none too bright, shows us how neophilia works and what it's for. One day, when he was sick in bed, the boy was given a compass to fiddle with to keep him occupied. The new plaything made him wonder about magnetic fields, which got him interested in physics, and, well, you know the rest. Few of us are Einsteins, but all of us have that same capacity to be curious about something new that sparks the learning and sustained interest that lead to achievements great and small.

To set the stage for the story of how neophilia helped to make us who we are, we need to revisit the tumultuous African milieu in which we evolved. A brief stop at the National Mall in Washington, D.C., orients us for the journey.

PART ONE

# Neophilia and Us

# One

# How We Became
# Who We Are

*There is always something new out of Africa.*

—Pliny the Elder, *Natural History*

ANYONE SEEKING PROOF that neophilia can lead us to glorious achievements need look no further than the National Air and Space Museum. High above your head in the spectacular entry hall soar legendary aircraft, including Charles Lindbergh's *Spirit of St. Louis.* (The 1903 Wright flyer, which was the world's first plane, has its own department upstairs, where you learn that Wilbur and Orville's Ohio clan also advanced new social causes such as abolition and women's rights—innovation of a different kind.) It's the manned spacecraft, however, that offer the most dramatic testimony to our genius for exploration and invention. "America is now a space-faring nation, a frontier good for millions of years," said James S. McDonnell, the pioneering aviation entrepreneur. "The only time remotely comparable was when Columbus discovered a whole new world." Most of these vessels are nothing like the gleaming ships in *Star Trek* or *Battlestar Galactica*, being much smaller, funkier, and more fragile seeming than you'd expect. In fact, many look exactly like the made-in-the-garage, figuring-this-out-as-we-go-along contraptions that they are—an especially poignant quality considering their unfathomable destinations and precious cargo.

As you travel through the National Mall to the Smithsonian Institution's Natural History Museum and enter its new Hall of Human Origins, you might well recall the famous opening scene in *2001: A Space Odyssey*, in which a pensive primate tosses into the sky a bone that morphs into an orbital satellite. The user-friendly hall offers profound insights into the origins of the neophilia that inspired both experiments. Its exhibits, from touchable fossils to flickering video campfires, have been carefully choreographed by Richard Potts, the paleoanthropologist who directs the human origins program, to illustrate what scientists call the theory of variability selection. A prominent sign by the hall's entry neatly summarizes this cutting-edge perspective on our evolution, which emphasizes its environmental dynamics: "Humans evolved in response to a changing world."

Understanding how neophilia became integral to who we are requires some background on the volatile time and place in which we evolved. Despite recent powerful reminders like the Japanese tsunami, the Haitian earthquake, and Iceland's volcanic eruption, as well as our increasingly peculiar weather, it's easy for us urbanized, temperature-controlled, postindustrial folk to forget that we've always lived on an unpredictable planet that, with a sneeze or a shrug, can still thwart our plans and devastate our ranks as it has so often in the past.

Six million years ago, in our turbulent African nursery, our earliest prehuman ancestors were already becoming better equipped to deal with nature's slings and arrows. Because they had developed the ability to stand erect on their stubby legs, they could find and reach more food—a major asset for survival. Our 3.2-million-year-old Ethiopian precursor Lucy, who's represented in one of the hall's dioramas, was a kind of primate ATV who could both walk upright and travel through the trees. By 2.5 million years ago, *Homo habilis*, one of the earliest members of the human genus, made tools and scavenged big animals for high-protein meat. About 2 million years ago, *Homo erectus* walked fully upright with a smooth stride, which enabled easier travel and better access to edibles as well as enhanced the ability to carry tools and babies, communicate with facial expressions, and intimidate four-footed predators. (We're still paying the price for this handy bipedalism with our fallen arches, tricky knees, and bad backs, to say nothing of the world's biggest butts, created by these ancestors' repositioned pelvic muscles.) By 500,000 years ago, our distant forebears' brains had tripled to nearly modern size, enabling them to crunch more information faster and dream up better survival strategies.

Geological and climatological evidence shows that we slowly evolved into a separate species during a time of extraordinarily violent environmental upheavals. Between 800,000 and 200,000 years ago, Africa was wracked by droughts and monsoons, expanding glaciers and volcanic eruptions. Organisms struggling to survive in such shifting and often inhospitable environments have two choices: they can migrate in hopes of finding the kind of setting they are used to or adjust to the new conditions. Many creatures, including a number of early human species very much like us, stuck with doing things the same old way in the same old neighborhood and simply died out.

*Homo sapiens* emerged from this seething environmental cauldron as a distinct species and nature's supreme neophile around 195,000 years ago. These early humans, who would physically blend right in at the local Cineplex, were well equipped for the exploration and risk taking, learning and creating that life in their challenging environments demanded. Most important, they had the world's largest brain relative to body size: a neurological supercomputer that could process huge amounts of information quickly, which is a great advantage in new situations. (Once again, however, there's no free lunch. Our copious gray matter hogs 20 percent of the body's total energy, and the bony skull that protects it causes painful, risky childbirth.) Unlike their inflexible extinct cousins, our adaptable forebears could skillfully tailor their behavior to changing circumstances. As Potts puts it, "They hunkered down and tried to accommodate new situations by figuring out what new things they had to do in order to survive."

Our ancestors' neophilia was boosted by their modern nervous system's sophisticated circuitry for the regulation of dopamine. One of the brain's major chemical messengers that mediate our emotional responses to the world, this neurotransmitter is particularly important to the seeking and processing of both novelty and rewards. In fact, our dopaminergic differences help explain why some of us are eager to explore new horizons, while others focus on the risks involved.

Imagine a group of these early relatives trying to figure out the best survival scheme in one of their wild and woolly environments. The neophiliacs urge fording the wide, turbulent river to see if there are better resources on the other side, to say nothing of how much they'd enjoy the white-water thrills involved. The neophobes object. They point out that at least they know what dangers they face on their familiar turf and argue for staying put and making the best of it. Most of the gang are moderate neophiles, who listen to these arguments, weigh the fear of risk against the hope of reward, and search for the best plan. These three groups may have needed some grooming and tailoring, but their modern successors are invariably in evidence at business conferences, PTA meetings, political conventions, and other gatherings, sometimes including the family dinner table.

Scientists increasingly resist making hard distinctions between the behavioral effects of nature and nurture—that is, biology and environment, or experience. The archaeological record duly shows that our neophilia arose from the interaction between our physiological development and the cultural sort, particularly our increasing skill at passing down the new things we learned and created. As we got better at sheer survival, we could afford to direct more of our novelty seeking to higher pursuits. The many artifacts from about 110,000 years ago onward offer strong testimony to our forebears' growing social, intellectual, and creative abilities. By 70,000 years ago, they were not only surviving, learning, and innovating but also displaying human civilization's great hallmark: the sharing and accumulation of sophisticated knowledge.

Between 80,000 and 70,000 years ago, the flexibility and inventiveness that bespeak our physically and culturally primed neophilia saved *Homo sapiens* from extinction. Starting about 135,000 years ago, Africa was roiled by a period of particularly cataclysmic environmental change. Geological samples drilled from lake cores convince Potts and others that the major problem was a series of megadroughts that turned even fathomless lakes into dry holes and eventually decimated the human population. Scientists argue over the number of adults left to reproduce, offering estimates that range from ten thousand "breeders" to two thousand to a mere six hundred. As a result of this so-called bottleneck, or restriction in genetic diversity, all of us walking the earth today are descended from this small group, which explains our strong genetic similarity, the recently discovered odd *soupçon* of Western Neanderthal and Asian Denisovan material notwithstanding.

Thanks to their ability to cope with new and shifting situations, a small remnant of the human race had managed to survive catastrophic environmental change by finding ways to adapt to conditions as they arose. About 70,000 years ago, an era of remarkable environmental stability allowed this beleaguered but wiser population to recover and increase. Nevertheless, says Potts, "any way you cut it, we were an endangered species. We almost bit the dust. It's astonishing that we had evolved sufficient resilience to expand out of that difficult time."

ANTHROPOLOGISTS ESSENTIALLY AGREE about the major milestones in our evolutionary saga thus far in our story. *Homo sapiens* had become fully modern in behavior as well as physiology. Like us, these forebears formed tightly bonded groups and secure home bases that fostered children's prolonged dependence and learning. They lived in the stable, sizable, sociable communities connected to other bands and the larger world that support inventiveness and the sharing of knowledge. Around 50,000 to 40,000 years ago, however, they became particularly busy exploring and innovating.

Large populations left Africa for good and dispersed into Europe and Asia. (Later groups would reach North America between 20,000 and 15,000 years ago and South America between 15,000 and 12,000 years ago.) Human fossils found in Israel and China prove that we had the skills to explore distant new environments as early as 130,000 to 100,000 years ago, but these later migrations were of an utterly different magnitude, both in size and consequences. Intriguingly, about 40,000 years ago, *Homo sapiens* also ignited a "creative explosion." This prehistoric combination of the Industrial Revolution and the Renaissance yielded much more sophisticated tools and art, culminating in the famous French and Spanish cave paintings done between 32,000 and 18,000 years ago.

The testimony that the great migrations and creative explosion offer to our species' increasingly sophisticated neophilia is incontrovertible, but anthropologists argue about its source. Advocates of the "sudden and recent" school of behavioral evolution suspect biological change. They propose that around 50,000 to 40,000 years ago, another still mysterious catastrophe, such as extreme aridity, stimulated the success, or accumulation, of certain mutations. These genetic variants helped to modernize human behavior in general and the novelty seeking apparent in the migrations and inventive brilliance in particular. (This theory is discussed in more depth in chapter 5.)

Members of the "slow and early" school of behavioral evolution, including Potts, attribute our growing success at adapting to environmental change and our increasing explorativeness and artistry not to biology but to culture—especially the sharing and building of knowledge. They refuse to attribute a complex behavior such as novelty seeking or creativity to a single gene, although they don't rule out the possibility that mutations could have enhanced our neophilic capacities at some point. According to their scenario, around 300,000 to 250,000 years ago, our ancestors began a long, incremental transition to our basic way of life, which was in place at least by 70,000 to 60,000 years ago. Seen in this light, the great migrations and sophisticated artworks simply prove that we had developed the skills required to travel far from our African nest at will and to make things that were beautiful and meaningful as well as useful.

To the slow-and-early scientists, who stress the importance

of environmental dynamics in our evolution, the artistry so apparent in the later European cave paintings was probably fostered by the crowding caused by people fleeing from the era's advancing glaciers. Such an increase in a population's density also increased the chances that bright ideas might catch on, be shared and elaborated on, last over time, and "pile up with other innovations," says Potts. "To my mind, that accumulation is the key to the creative explosion and what has made human beings culturally so distinct."

A paleoanthropologist at New York City's American Museum of Natural History, Ian Tattersall offers yet a third variation on the theme of how we became who we are. He asserts that although our major behavioral leaps since emerging as a species have typically been triggered by cultural responses to the environment rather than biology, these breakthroughs have occurred sporadically rather than gradually. For that matter, he says, "even birds didn't use their feathers to fly for many millions of years after they had acquired them." Similarly, our remote ancestors first used fire in the domestic sense about 800,000 years ago, but they didn't begin to employ it regularly until some 400,000 years later. "Things can lie fallow till someone picks up on a use for them," he says. "For a very long time, our pattern has been that nothing much happens in between technological leaps, sometimes for hugely extended periods, until the next radical idea comes along."

To Tattersall, the surging explorativeness and inventiveness apparent in the great migrations and creative explosions are best explained by our belated discovery of our capacity for symbolic thought. Big-brained *Homo sapiens* had the necessary neurological wherewithal for processing the world in abstract ways such as writing, maps, and stories when we debuted about 195,000 years ago, but we didn't exploit that potential till much later. By 75,000 years ago, says Tattersall, "we see stirrings of people beginning to discover their cognitive possibilities and manipulate information about the world in a new way."

Anthropologists have only recently recognized the fact that a great idea whose time has come tends to occur not just to a lone genius but independently to neophiles in many places. Thus, Tattersall thinks that our latent capacity for symbolic thinking was unleashed at some point after 100,000 years ago, when one or more populations spontaneously invented language, which then spread rapidly to other groups. "The capacity for symbolic perception was there," he says, "but the behavior wasn't, until language released it. One innovation often leads to another, and if you have the neuronal wiring for language, sooner or later you'll come to symbolic thinking."

Our own recent ability to capture the knowledge of the ages in a series of ones and zeros is the latest illustration of our capacity for symbolic thought, but its greatest manifestation— and the ultimate form of neophilia—is the creation of our individual inner worlds. "That's what distinguishes us from all other organisms," says Tattersall. "They pretty much live in the world that nature presents to them. They react to it with various degrees of sophistication, but they don't remake it in their heads. Our symbolic ability lets us imagine the world as it is or as it might be—to ask 'What if?'"

Just as symbolic thinking arises from language, Tattersall suspects, our neophilia arises from symbolic thought. "I think our novelty-seeking ability is an effect, not a cause. It's a by-product of the fact that we're able to create new worlds in our heads. It's the general ability to do *that* from which everything else comes."

ANTHROPOLOGISTS MAY WRANGLE over the degrees to which nature and nurture were responsible, but there's no argument about our early forebears' ever more skillful engagement with the new and different. A look at what we were up to about 30,000 years ago, around the time that our close cousin *Homo neanderthalensis* died out, tells the tale. These bright, brawny relatives, like their mysterious cousins the Denisovans, emerged in Africa as a separate species about 500,000 years ago. The Neanderthals settled in Europe and the Near East, while the Denisovans moved into Asia.

The Neanderthals were like us in many ways. They were more sturdily built than we are, and even their faces were heavier than our own childlike visages, which may stimulate bonding and caring. However, they had big brains, made good tools and even some symbolic artifacts, and exploited their local resources proficiently. The most important difference between them and us was their preference for sticking to a specific kind of environment versus our flexibility. As

Potts says, "They were the cold-adapted specialists on our family tree."

Like the early African *Homo* groups that had suited themselves to forests or deserts and then disappeared when those ecological niches vanished, the Neanderthals were relative neophobes. They rarely traveled more than fifty miles, for example and, unlike *Homo sapiens*, groups didn't communicate much with each other. When they headed back up into northern Europe after one of the great glacial expansions, a big surprise awaited. By about 40,000 years ago, unlike the conservative, clannish Neanderthals, *Homo sapiens*'s enterprising, sociable groups were exchanging resources and forging alliances with one another as far as five hundred kilometers away, right on the edges of Europe. Some 10,000 years later, we had penetrated the Neanderthals' northern stomping grounds and perhaps supplied the competition that helped to extinguish them.

That we tall, slim, baby-faced, sun-worshipping Africans survived and perhaps conquered in the frosty environment of the rugged, cold-adapted Neanderthals is powerful proof of our genius for adapting to the new and different. Our sophisticated technology enabled us to thrive in frigid or tropical climes alike. Our heavy-duty cousins made loose clothing by using stone awls to punch holes in skins, for example, but our sewing needles allowed us to create much warmer tailored garments that closely fit the body. As Potts says, "When we came onto the scene that they were specialized for, we already had a cultural buffering system to help us through hard times."

. . .

ONE EXHIBIT IN THE Hall of Human Origins is such a hit with visitors that the Smithsonian offers a smartphone app version. After waiting in a long line for your turn, you sit before a screen that scans your face, then modifies your *Homo sapiens* features into the visage of one of six other fellow hominins, as anthropologists now call early humans and their near relations. All are extinct, but at least three of these intelligent cousins coexisted with us: *Homo neanderthalensis*, *Homo erectus*, and hobbitlike *Homo floresiensis*, which died out a mere 17,000 years ago. Their faces, so like yet unlike ours, evoke John Dryden: "Not Heav'n itself upon the past has pow'r; / But what has been has been, and I have had my hour."

As you watch your features and hairline shift on the magic screen, you feel a surprising connection with these relatives who lived in a time so remote that we vaguely call it "prehistoric." All around you is the physical evidence of the peculiar talent for adapting to the unfamiliar and unexpected that helped to transform the likes of them to the likes of us, gazing at them in a museum. You wonder over this long process of becoming . . . what?

As we've moved from the epoch of the hunter-gatherers— the vast majority of our time as a species—to the agricultural, industrial, and information ages, our neophilia has changed and developed with us. Remarking on a phenomenon that strikes him as unusual, at least in evolutionary terms, Tattersall says, "The degree to which modern humans seek new things and invent new technology to respond to new situations is very clearly expressed in our lives now."

One obvious factor in the spikes in both novelty and neophilia in the West since the eighteenth century is that most of us no longer have to live on a survival level. Our inventiveness needn't be focused on our safety, food, clothing, and shelter. As Potts says, "I wonder how much of the novelty-seeking aspect of our cognitive and social makeup results from the fact that we have a lot more leisure time now than we used to, but we still have this brain and social makeup that feed off of novelty. So maybe our cognitive and social behavior is an artifact of our conditions now. That doesn't minimize our novelty seeking but shows how much of a need and desire it is."

Evolution doesn't predict the future very well, but one thing is plain: To survive and thrive, *Homo sapiens* must keep adapting to a world of constant change. However, our capacity for handling new things is increasingly being tested by an unprecedented explosion of them. Figuring out how to respond to this embarrassment of riches by becoming more productive rather than more distracted is easier if you understand a few basics of how and why your brain reacts to new things.

*Two*

# Surprise Detector

YOU HAVE ONLY TO FOLLOW a crawling baby around for a while to see that right from the beginning, we're intrinsically motivated to check out something new or different just because, as climber George Mallory said of Mount Everest, "it is there." An inventive experiment offers scientific testimony to novelty's riveting power. Earlier studies of the "weapons focus effect" had shown that the presence of a gun—a highly arousing stimulus—at a crime scene attracted bystanders' attention so strongly that their memory of the larger situation was impaired, thus rendering their much-vaunted eyewitness testimony unreliable. In a later experiment, however, some canny psychologists showed that simply replacing the gun with a piece of celery in an otherwise identical setting commanded people's attention as powerfully as the weapon. In other words, "What's that vegetable doing there?" draws your focus as readily as "Yikes! A gun!" This finding is yet another indication that your perception of the world is less an objective duplication of reality than a somewhat modified version that's often biased by your focus on anything new or unexpected.

The main reason you're drawn to the novel or surprising is that it could upset the safe, predictable status quo and the game plan you've based on it, perhaps even jeopardizing your survival. If you've ever tried to carry on a conversation in a room in which a TV is playing, you know that it's hard not to glance at the screen occasionally. Even if you don't want to watch, your brain is attracted by that constantly shifting stream of images, because change can have life-or-death consequences. Indeed, if our early African ancestors hadn't been good at zeroing in on the just-ripened fruit or the looming predators, we wouldn't be here. For the same reason, a keen sensitivity to the odd detail that doesn't quite jibe with the way things usually are or ought to be is a major asset for a soldier in a war zone or a Secret Service agent in a crowd. Even in everyday situations, you can't afford to miss that jaywalker darting in front of your car or the single new and important fact in a long, boring list.

The brain is conventionally portrayed as a kind of wet computer, or information processor, but some intriguing research suggests that "surprise detector" might be a better description. To investigate what influences our critical decisions of where to look next, Laurent Itti, a computational neuroscientist at the University of Southern California, and his collaborator, Pierre Baldi of the University of California at Irvine, first prescreened videotapes for the locations of any sudden changes or unexpected events. Then they asked volunteers to watch the films while being monitored by eye-tracking machines. Most of the time, the team found, their subjects focused on the place that offered something new or unexpected.

The idea of the brain as a surprise detector has interesting technological as well as behavioral implications. The current generation of computers is based on information theory's quantitative, objective approach to data. If the brain is qualitatively biased to the new and surprising, however, as his research suggests, "the attempt to quantify information is not appropriate for human thought processes and mental operations," says Itti. "This perspective ignores the fact that most information, from your sensory organs' input to the content of all too many e-mail attachments, is boring, irrelevant, and useless." (Indeed, one major reason a robot isn't already driving your car for you is that these clever tools still can't detect and react to rapidly changing traffic conditions as well as your novelty-oriented brain can.) A new breed of computers that uses surprise as its main operating principle could help filter the fresh, interesting stuff from the floods of electronic data you get each day—a major concern of the ongoing information revolution.

Seen in the light of this research, the brain isn't just an

impartial data cruncher but a novelty-seeking machine that helps us understand the world by selectively focusing us on its newest, most interesting bits and pieces. After all, says Itti, with philosophical Gallic flair, "What else could we be seeking?"

TO SURVIVE, you must be aroused by the new and different. To be efficient and productive, however, you must focus your finite mental energy and attention on those novel sights and sounds, thoughts and feelings that somehow matter and screen out the rest. Just as arousal alerts and orients you to new things, the complementary process of adaptation helps you filter out the unimportant ones.

Neophilia arises from this dual dynamic of getting excited by something new and then getting used to it, which frees and perhaps even spurs you to search for the next stimulus. Psych 101 usually includes a classic experiment that demonstrates living creatures' preference for stimulation over boredom. In one such study, caged monkeys worked for hours to pick a lock simply for the sheer joy of having something interesting to do. In another, they pressed a lever to open a window that allowed them to peer into others' cages or watch a toy train chugging around its tracks. Like our fellow primates, we'll work just to be excited by the new rather than dulled by the old, which has spurred achievements from mapping the globe to inventing the symphony.

"Attentional blink" experiments show how arousal and adaptation affect your attention and experience in daily life.

Suppose that you've volunteered for a study in which you're asked to respond to a series of letters. If an anomalous image, say, of a face, suddenly appears in the sequence, your "sticky," or prolonged, focus on that unexpected cue—a sign of arousal and increased cognitive processing—will cause you to blink and miss the next few letters. The second time around, however, the picture is less surprising, and you'll barely notice it. By the third go-round, you'll have adapted to the face so thoroughly that you won't waste your time and attention by reacting to it at all.

Arousal by and adaptation to novelty are so essential to survival that newborn babies less than a day old will stare at a new image for about forty-one seconds, then tune it out when repeated showings render it boring. For that matter, even a humble visual neuron, or nerve cell, exhibits the same dynamic. Imagine that it begins to get dark while you're working at your desk, so you turn on your lamp. The suddenly brighter red of that apple beside your coffee mug will arouse and activate the neurons in charge of monitoring that bit of your visible world. If your office's lighting stays constant for a while, however, those nerve cells will adapt and quiet down until the next change. The neurons' "motivation" in this minuscule drama is the same as yours on a vastly larger scale: to stay on top of important new developments in their domain and tune out the humdrum, so that they're ready to respond appropriately to whatever happens next.

All day long, as you go about your business, you're aroused by and then adapt to new things. First, you're excited by that tangy sauce, smell of smoke, or e-mail *ping*. You perk up, zero in, and check this fresh information against the knowledge of the world that's stored in your working memory. If you decide that this new stimulus merits further engagement, you take another taste, check for fire, or read the message. Should you deem the cue unimportant, you adapt to it, which consigns it to the wallpaper of your world and thus enables you to get back to the business at hand.

This sequence of getting excited by something new and then getting used to it is responsible for a phenomenon that underlies some very pleasant and unpleasant experiences, which scientists in different fields call the "novelty effect." To psychologists who study stress, this dynamic explains why your first encounter with a negative event—a steep hike in your utility rates, say, or your teenager's *D* in algebra—produces the highest excitation, which decreases over time with subsequent high bills and poor math grades. In biology, the "Coolidge effect" is the strong mammalian tendency to get aroused by and then adapt to a new sex partner. The label derives from a visit that the taciturn President Calvin Coolidge and his wife allegedly paid to a farm. When Mrs. Coolidge professed amazement at the number of fertile eggs produced with the cooperation of a very few roosters, the farmer explained that his doughty cocks each mated many times daily. The first lady said, "Tell that to Mr. Coolidge." In response, the president asked if each rooster only mounted the same hen. On the contrary, said the farmer, each male's partners were many and various. "Tell *that* to Mrs. Coolidge," said the president.

The novelty effect also plays an important role in innovation. (Indeed, it's impossible to separate newness from creativity, which, when stripped of smoke and mirrors, is simply the production of an original, useful idea.) Merely introducing something novel into the schoolroom or workplace, such as the latest electronic gadgetry, will improve the occupants' performance until the thrill wears off. Then too, many creative breakthroughs are sparked by the arousal provided by a fresh stimulus. Einstein only arrived at the special theory of relativity's ultimate *Aha!* after he left the office and boarded a streetcar; as it passed Bern's landmark clock tower, he realized that time can tick at different rates depending on how fast you move. Similarly, had Isaac Newton not left his accustomed quarters at Cambridge University for the different surroundings of his family's rural property, he wouldn't have noticed that fateful apple that fell to the ground and released the theory of universal gravitation.

Underscoring the stimulating role that a new environmental cue can play, psychologist Dean Simonton, who studies creativity at the University of California at Davis, observes that even Archimedes didn't experience his archetypal *Eureka!* until he stepped away from his desk and into his overflowing tub: "All of his work on the problem of buoyancy could not do what that bath did, and he was the greatest mathematician of the ancient world. Sometimes, you just need the missing piece of the puzzle, and something that seems irrelevant can lead you to a major discovery. A change of venue—taking a walk or breaking for a meal—means new stimuli, one of which may show you the way."

Creative breakthroughs sometimes also spring from a failure to adapt to a stimulus, which allows it to retain its novel, arousing quality. "Genius hits a target no one else can see," said Schopenhauer, and some of those targets are right under our noses. Many inventive people in diverse fields share an almost childlike ability to perceive arousing new facets in even the most familiar things, and, as Simonton says, "when you start asking questions about stuff that most people take for granted, you may end up with answers that no one imagined."

It's no accident that Lakshminarayanan Mahadevan, who's a professor of applied mathematics at Harvard, teaches a freshman seminar called "The Science of Everyday Life." In 2009, he won a MacArthur Foundation "genius grant" for figuring out common natural phenomena—why flags flutter, say, and how flowers bloom—then translating those mechanisms into mathematical principles that have applications in science, manufacturing, and other fields. His observations on the way in which honey pours and pools could help geologists understand the earth's molten core, for example, just as his analysis of why insects are able to walk on the ceiling might lead to new kinds of adhesives. Mahadevan calls his curiosity-driven approach to understanding the world an "old-school, very unfashionable way of doing science that used to be called 'natural philosophy' a century ago, where you wondered about everything. . . . Just because something is familiar doesn't mean you understand it. This is the common fallacy that all adults make and no child ever does."

To researchers who investigate factors that contribute to our quality of life, the skillful exploitation of the novelty effect can help us wring more enjoyment as well as more productivity from daily experience. The late economist Tibor Scitovsky, who studied the relationship between happiness and consumerism, argued that buying lots of inexpensive "pleasures"—arousing, gratifying things that, like a fresh bouquet or a great piece of chocolate, always evoke a *wow*—is a better investment in your quality of life than spending on "comforts," or more serious, usually more expensive things like kitchen appliances that you soon take for granted. You can also enjoy more *ooh-la-la*'s if you take a short break during a pleasurable event. Like an intermission at a concert, a pause during lovemaking or a break for a glass of water during a massage interrupts the adaptation process, so you can reexperience the arousal of the activity's novel delights.

LIKE ALL FORMS OF BEHAVIOR, excitation and adaptation not only confer benefits but can also cause problems, particularly at the extremes. Where arousal is concerned, we're hypersensitive to new things that could threaten our well-being. This self-protective "negativity bias" makes perfect evolutionary and practical sense regarding tornadoes, bounced checks, and fights. The downside, however, is that we can end up spending a lot of time being upset for what turns out to be no good reason.

Encounters with a person of a different race—for many, still a relatively novel stimulus—that become needlessly fraught are a good example of counterproductive negative arousal. Certain brain structures activate on these occasions, says Michael

Inzlicht, a social neuroscientist at the University of Toronto who studies stereotyping, but the reason for this excitation is unclear. However, if person A feels like a target of prejudice, as the only black, white, gay, or female person in a setting might, A becomes aroused and more vigilant, looking for indicators of bias that might not even be there. Responding to A's edgy demeanor, person B, who may harbor no prejudice, might end up feeling unjustly cast as a bigot. On the simplest level, as Inzlicht says, "all of this distress takes up a lot of time that could be spent doing other things." The consequences can also be more serious, especially for A, because people who feel stereotyped are likely to perform less well than they would if they were with others like themselves.

Like arousal, adaptation is subject to some kinks. An anxious person can't get used to a worry—a fear of flying, perhaps, or public speaking—and becomes preoccupied by it. A hoarder stays aroused by utterly boring objects such as bottle caps and rubber bands, reacting to them as if they were novel instead of dismissing them. Then, too, some of us adapt to stimulating things that, being dangerous, should have remained highly arousing.

The downside of getting used to something we shouldn't is neatly summed up by an axiom from wildlife management: "A fed bear is a dead bear." The big predators that roam in many large state and national parks can grow all too accustomed to campers and their carelessly stored food, which may result in dangerous encounters, maulings, and the adapted animal's destruction. Then, too, certain people who spend a lot of time in wild places can adapt to the normally highly arousing presence of large wild animals. In June 2010, Erwin Evert, a skilled botanist and outdoorsman, was killed by a grizzly near Yellowstone National Park after he ignored warnings and signs that a drugged "trouble bear" had just been released in the remote area. Stunned by this instance of adaptation gone awry, a shocked friend said, "What he's doing is walking toward the trap site. He knew it. Why he did it nobody can fully explain."

THE EXPLOSION OF novelty in the contemporary world has greatly accelerated the dynamics of arousal and adaptation, and thus the cycle of change, on the social as well as the individual level. We now get used to and over the latest, hottest thing almost as soon as we get excited by it. The top ten movies, DVDs, and music downloads are apt to shift every week, not because of improvements in quality but simply because they're new. If something is to sustain your interest in this culture of been there, done that, it must somehow delay or short-circuit the adaptation process. One way to effect that is what MIT anthropologist Grant McCracken calls "throwing something into the signal that doesn't quite make sense."

Our brains constantly sort information into conceptual categories: good or bad, rock or country, male or female. However, the things that most arouse us now increasingly resist such easy classification by incorporating an element of novelty in the form of uncertainty. Giving William James a postmodern spin, McCracken says, "We don't want things that are totally anomalous or odd, because they're just distressing, but those that somehow evade or stretch the category to which they might belong. We want things that we can't get at once, because we don't have a ready category for them, a way to think about them."

This novel "huh?" quality that sustains arousal and delays adaptation underlies the recent commercial appeal of the counterintuitive. Books get titles inspired by the best-selling *Everything Bad Is Good for You,* and trendy advertising agencies present dorky minivans as hot sports cars and Silicon Valley geeks as rock stars. Our reaction to the hip new cultural stimuli that tweak the arousal-adaptation process to keep us guessing reminds McCracken of that of a spider who feels its web tremble. "It goes, 'Oh, that's interesting!' What makes something interesting now is that it's ever so slightly counterexpectational." First, he says, comes the excitement: "This doesn't quite compute, and that's intriguing." Then, the prolongation of the decision to adapt or not: "Is this just noise in the system to dismiss? Or is it an opportunity to revise my categories?"

The new breed of cable TV shows specializes in feeding your uncertainty and challenging your categories. These programs arouse you with a surprising stimulus, let you start to get used to it, then make sure that it excites you again and keeps you guessing. When you tune in to *True Blood* for the first time, for example, you assume that vampires are the blood-sucking fiends of yore. Then, as you adapt to them, you start to feel that these unusual beings have just been misunderstood. When Bill Compton, the gentlemanly vamp next door, diffidently asks his girlfriend to provide a daily snack, you think, "How, er, sweet!" Then he or one of his dark cohorts does something so monstrous that you're back to square one again. McCracken bases the bets on his blog about which new shows will and won't work on their novel quirkiness. He's already bored by the prospect of a traditional buddy-cop show about to premiere: "How tedious! I don't even have to watch to know how every episode will play out. What I want is cop show meets . . . warlocks or something."

Ever since Ecclesiastes dissed the ancient Athenians for always "seeking some new thing," neophilia has been criticized in some quarters as a shallow search for quick and easy arousal. McCracken takes a more sanguine view. "Some people don't like it, but there's a growing number of us who love novelty and the chance to revisit our usual ways of thinking. That's the fun of it!" He quotes the French geographer Fernand Braudel: "Can it have been merely by coincidence that the future was to belong to the societies fickle enough to care about changing the colors, materials and shapes of costume, as well as the social order and the map of the world—societies, that is, which were ready to break with their traditions? There is a connection."

THE NEWSPAPER'S GOSSIP COLUMN invariably provides evidence that the process of getting excited by the new, then getting bored with it and searching for a fresh source of arousal, can jeopardize marital fidelity, sobriety, and other types of good behavior. However, the obituaries show that the novelty effect can also spur lives of great achievement. When Ari Kiev, a social psychiatrist at Cornell Medical College, died in 2009, his obit aptly observed that he "showed signs of intellectual restlessness early on." As a young doctor, he first investigated nontraditional African and Asian healing practices, then moved on to work on depression and suicide prevention. His interest in improving his patients' self-reliance and assertiveness next led him to investigate peak performance and the psychological hurdles that obstruct it. After writing several books on the subject and tutoring elite sports and business figures in his techniques, Kiev served as an expert witness in court cases and decided to earn a degree in law. By the time he died at the age of seventy-five, this easily bored intellectual neophiliac had managed to lead not just one but several exciting and productive professional lives.

The fundamental processes of arousal and adaptation are vital to all creatures' survival. For us, however, they also provide the foundation for our much subtler, more sophisticated emotions. These mind-body states of feeling enable us to respond more flexibly to the world in general and the new and different in particular.

If you suddenly spot a man from Mars while walking down the street with two friends, all of you will be excited by the sheer novelty. Then your adventurous pal, who's more curious than afraid, might draw closer for a better look, while your anxious companion beats a retreat, and you stay put to monitor the situation further. Similarly, one buddy may be an enthusiastic early adopter of the latest miracle phone, while the other shrinks back from the learning required and you wait for the cheaper, glitch-free next generation.

Whether someone finds the Martian or the gadget thrilling, chilling, or something in between bespeaks three distinctive emotional and motivational reactions to novelty—*approach, avoid,* and *maybe*—that color how neophiliacs, neophobes, and neophiles see the world and live their lives.

*Three*

# Approach, Avoid, or Maybe

O<small>NCE YOU'RE AROUSED</small> by an unfamiliar sight or sound, thought or feeling that could affect your well-being, you face a decision: Should you approach it, flee from it, or continue to evaluate it? Your choice will be influenced by certain positive and/or negative emotions that the stimulus elicits in you. Whether it's "Wow!" "Uh-oh!" or "Hmm," your characteristic way of reacting to new things across time and many circumstances is the major ingredient in your emotional response to the world and your personality.

The three upbeat, underappreciated feelings of surprise, curiosity, and interest, which motivate us to approach new things that seem promising, form neophilia's affective foundation. Because they inspire us to learn and often seem more like thoughts, they're called the "knowledge emotions." The simplest is the brief, superficial, archaic *Oh!* evoked by the popping of a balloon or the unanticipated sight of a long-lost friend. (For additional information, please see *Notes*.) This initial response to the novel or unexpected requires little in the way of intelligence or knowledge. Indeed, a newborn's response is the same as an adult's. The next steps up from fleeting surprise are the more sustained feelings of curiosity and interest. If we fail to follow their lead and explore new things, like the Chinese farmers in the fable who thought the only way to roast a pig was to burn down the building around it, we're doomed to allow the past to determine our present and future.

Like a sip of champagne, bubbly curiosity lifts us out of quotidian reality and a business-as-usual mind-set and slips us into the *approach* reaction to the unfamiliar: What's tai chi like? Where is that wonderful scent coming from? How's the food at that Turkish restaurant? We tend to use *curiosity* for the imminent or short-lived experience—"What's that funny-looking bird?"—and *interest* for one that's more abiding—"I've joined the Audubon Club"—but the two terms describe the same novelty-oriented emotional state.

A few moments of playing peekaboo demonstrate that the level of novelty that captivates an infant is so basic as to be comical. Nevertheless, as Paul Silvia, a psychologist who studies the knowledge emotions at the University of North Carolina at Greensboro, observes, "The reason babies can be surprised is so that they can be interested, which is the more important thing functionally and adaptively. They have to learn absolutely fricking *everything*, and interest is the engine for that."

Of course, that educational process never really stops, and the knowledge emotions continue to be the carrots on the stick that drive us down the life-long road of learning and achievement. After all, says Silvia, "if you couldn't get interested in new things, you'd constantly be afraid, because you'd freak out every time one came along." Whether you're drawn to explore the great outdoors or the great books, he says, "by becoming more curious and interested in life, you'll also have a more curious and interesting life."

The biographies of notably creative people invariably reveal driven individuals whose *approach* reaction to learning new things enabled them to accumulate the bits and pieces of insight they needed to make their major breakthroughs. (For additional information, please see *Notes*.) Fictional and cinematic accounts may portray great discoveries as thunderbolts from the blue, but, in fact, they're built on a solid foundation of curiosity-inspired learning and years of hard work. That's why there are pint-sized prodigies in music, where the basics are readily acquired, but not in physics, where even a genius must spend many years mastering the essentials. Thus, the long journey toward the theory of relativity began in earnest when sixteen-year-old Einstein noticed a peculiarity that his scientific elders and betters had adapted to as unimportant, namely a certain disconnect between Newtonian mechanics and Maxwell's equations for electromagnetism. Instead of dismissing his observation, he set out to learn the physics and math that provided the springboard for the great leap to come many years later.

Arguably the patron saint of curiosity, Charles Darwin

made his celebrated "discovery" of evolution by natural selection not in a blinding flash but over decades of study, observation, and experimentation that produced many incremental insights. Isaac Newton was history's greatest scientist, but even he acknowledged the intellectual elbow grease that original thinking requires: "I keep the subject constantly before me and wait until the first dawnings open little by little before me into the full light."

The curiosity and interest aroused by a creative problem can not only motivate the learning required to solve it but can also lead you to reformulate the issue or even stumble onto a better one to investigate. The history of the elevator offers an amusing illustration of the importance of this neophilic process that psychologists call "problem finding," which is sometimes defined as "thinking about what to think about." At first, people were frustrated by the revolutionary lift's slow ascent of the new skyscrapers. Engineers duly tried to make elevators go faster, but the complaints continued. One day, a fellow with no such professional credentials thought for a few moments, then said, "Put mirrors around the doors and inside the cars." Once he had found the real problem—not the elevator's speed but the boredom that generated the riders' impatience—the solution was easy.

Speaking of innovative problem finding in his very different domain, Einstein said, "To raise new questions, new possibilities, to regard old problems from a new angle, requires creative imagination and marks real advance in science." That's standard operating procedure for Dr. Thomas Insel, a psychiatrist and neuroscientist who's the director of the

National Institute of Mental Health (NIMH), in Bethesda, Maryland. When he first arrived at this world-class center for the study of the brain and behavior in 1979, young Dr. Insel tackled a notoriously difficult, intractable problem from a very different angle indeed. Obsessive-compulsive disorder (OCD), which plagues its victims with relentlessly recurring thoughts—of dirtiness, say, or danger—and the behavioral rituals, such as repeated washing or checking, meant to ameliorate them, had long been regarded as a "neurosis" caused by "repressed hostility." However, Insel's curiosity was aroused by an odd similarity between OCD's repetitive symptoms and animals' instinctual grooming and nesting behavior. Following the line of inquiry suggested by this clue, he discovered the brain glitch that was responsible for these patients' misery and found a drug that often rapidly relieved it.

Instead of settling down comfortably in biological psychiatry, this intellectual neophile dived into the emerging field of neuroscience. When you learn a new discipline, Insel says, "that's when the best ideas, which are different from what people in your usual field think about, frequently jump up and hit you. It's like being a tourist who brings home new insights." After ten years of research, he discovered the neurochemical basis of bonding, or the attachment that forms between parents and infants or adult lovers. Next, his growing interest in evolutionary biology drew him to Atlanta's Yerkes National Primate Research Center, where he became fascinated with an entirely different domain: institutional administration, which he calls "creative leadership." That experience in turn led him back to the NIMH and its prestigious directorship.

Expressing neophilia's hallmarks of curiosity, sustained interest, zeal for learning, and openness to the unknown and uncertain, Insel says gleefully, "Almost everything I was taught as a grad student thirty years ago is now wrong. We're realizing that mental disorders are really brain problems, which gives us a lot of insight into how they must be handled. Our knowledge is so much more sophisticated now, including our knowledge of what we don't know."

JUST AS THE positive neophilic knowledge emotions urge you to explore, learn, and create rewarding new things, the negative neophobic feelings of anxiety and fear warn you to steer clear of those that seem risky. This *avoid* response stands you in good stead if you're in a dangerous neighborhood, say, or are tempted to go full steam ahead with your latest brainstorm before thinking it through. Indeed, creative people have not just more good new ideas but more ideas, period, many of which are bad. The great Romantic composer Robert Schumann tried to improve his piano skills by splinting one finger, which caused nerve damage that left him unable to play at all. More recently, Wall Street's geniuses plunged America into a devastating recession with their highly creative financial inventions, such as mortgage-backed securities.

Negative emotional responses to novelty can protect you from harm, but they can also discourage you from learning new things and pursuing potential rewards. All of us can look back regretfully at opportunities we failed to pursue out of fear. If only you hadn't been scared to try snorkeling on vacation, you could have seen a whole new world. If you hadn't worried about buying that great condo in a transitional neighborhood, you wouldn't be priced out of the market now. If you hadn't chickened out on that blind date, you could have ended up with the dreamboat.

The twenty-first-century college campus offers a dismaying and stunningly underremarked example of how anxiety about the risk associated with new ways of thinking can limit learning and stunt creativity. Virtually all the people quoted in these pages, many of whom are professors as well as researchers, bemoan the dramatic increase in the number of students who are reluctant to come up with fresh ideas, argue with their teachers, or otherwise challenge the status quo. Some blame this neophobic behavior on a fear of rocking the boat during a prolonged period of economic uncertainty and increased competition for jobs and other opportunities. Others point to a coddled generation's sense of entitlement to easy A's, and still others to some combination of both.

Whatever the reason for the increase in the young's *avoid* response to new ways of thinking, Trinity College's Barbara Benedict, who has studied curiosity's representation in literature, speaks for many academics in calling the phenomenon "extremely dispiriting, an outrage." Instead of challenging a professor's ideas, she says, "these young people want him or her to keep the authority figure's role straight, so they can keep their roles as A students straight. It's really *bad*." Daniel Pink, a writer and lecturer who chronicles the changing workplace, says that "it sometimes seems that the students' first response to new information is 'Will this be on the test?'

They aren't good risk managers. They overstate the risk of novelty and divergence, and they understate the risk of being compliant with authority figures. It's a colossal mistake—and frightening."

VIRTUALLY EVERYONE RECOILS in fear from novelty in the form of a rattlesnake on the trail or a crouched figure in a dark alley, because the danger is crystal clear. When something new evokes both your anxiety about risk and your hope of reward, however, the result is an emotional battle known as an "approach-avoidance conflict."

*Taking that job in a new city means a big raise, but what if I hate it there? The stranger at the bar is attractive, but suppose he's a weirdo? This start-up seems promising, but what if it flops? That Outward Bound trip sounds exciting, but what if it's too challenging for me?* Deciding to go for it and engage with the new prospect could reward you with a career boost, a lover, wealth, or an unforgettable vacation. On the other hand, you could end up miserable, scared, bankrupt, or embarrassed. Aside from a temperamentally fearless minority of us, says Silvia, "novelty and anxiety—you really can't have just one."

The *angst* caused by approach-avoidance conflicts is rooted in the fact that they frustrate your powerful need to control your own experience—a crucial factor in your mental health. When you don't feel in charge, you're vulnerable to the senses of hopelessness and helplessness that over time can spiral downward into depression. New things that create uncertainty about how to respond frustrate your desire for control by preventing the brain from doing its most important job: figuring out what you should do next. "What is anxiety, exactly?" says social neuroscientist Michael Inzlicht. "It's not fear, but worry, which results from a conflict between goals. The rat sees a nice piece of cheese, but also a cat in the distance. What to do? Knowing or not knowing how to respond—we're really primed to resolve that, and something new or uncertain can get in the way."

An interesting experiment on our pronounced negativity bias, or heightened sensitivity to possible threats, that was initially designed to test psychologist Roy Baumeister's famously economical assertion that "bad is stronger than good" ended up demonstrating just how upsetting novelty in the form of uncertainty can be. Inzlicht and his students asked their subjects to press a button one second after a visual cue appeared on a screen. If the volunteers performed accurately, they were shown a plus sign as a reward. If they didn't, they got a less gratifying minus sign. Almost as an afterthought, the researchers added what they assumed would serve as a kind of neutral control: a question mark that kept the volunteers from knowing whether they had succeeded or not. Then the team used EEG technology to monitor their subjects' very fast brain reactions to this positive, negative, or uninformative input.

As they pretty much expected, the EEG data showed that the minus sign's bad feedback was more arousing than the plus sign's good sort. However, the researchers were stunned to see that the presumably neutral question mark elicited a negative reaction just as intense as the minus sign's. "I don't want to anthropomorphize the brain," says Inzlicht, "but I'm convinced that *we're* biased both to novelty and uncertainty, and that we're more averse to uncertainty than is commonly thought. If bad is stronger than good, the unknown is just as strong as bad and possibly stronger."

Anyone who has waited for an exam grade, a callback after a job interview, or a biopsy result knows firsthand the distress we feel when uncertainty prevents us from getting on with our lives. "We have an epistemic drive to know, so we can understand, so we can predict, so we can do, and thus navigate through life," says Inzlicht. "We're built to reduce uncertainty in the service of providing explanations that lead to forecasts. To do that, however, we first have to know what's out there, which is why we key into unknowns."

Considering the magnitude of the financial stakes involved in their decisions, it's not surprising that like individuals, companies and many other organizations wrestle with the emotional approach-avoid conflicts sparked by the risk and uncertainty inherent in a new idea. In what he calls "an almost bipolar reaction," Pink says that a corporation passionately hopes to invent something that the world doesn't even know it's missing—say, a cool little flip video camera that's smaller than a pack of cigarettes and costs less than a hundred dollars—yet also fears that if it tries something new, the result could be a flop: "Large corporations that are answerable to shareholders who punish them severely in the short term especially don't like to make mistakes."

Creative companies and institutions, from the NIMH to Google, try to reduce the conflict generated by new ideas by providing what Pink calls "safe havens for failure." One Australian firm, for example, holds "FedEx" days, when employees get twenty-four hours to work on whatever they want to without permission, supervision, or censure, and then "deliver" the results to their colleagues the next day. This strategy of tapping the individual's intrinsic motivation to try something new is very popular with workers and has also generated many innovative ideas and products for the company. Despite the attendant *Sturm und Drang,* Pink says, "according to a theory called 'the edge of chaos,' the most dynamic spot to be is the place between order and the edge, where things are evolving, changing, and new."

In contrast to neophilic institutions' *approach* response to new ideas and the employees who come up with them, neophobic organizations incline toward an *avoid* reaction and tend to see their workers as naturally passive and disengaged. As Pink says, "That theory about human nature gets us into profound trouble. On the other hand, if we assume that it's human nature to be active and involved, then we have to learn passivity and inertia. Those two theories lead you down very different paths, especially regarding novelty."

A GLIMPSE AT HER multifaceted résumé makes clear which path Esther Dyson, who's best known as a pioneer in the field of information technology, has chosen. After a lackluster experience studying economics at Harvard—"They just wanted us to regurgitate stuff that was already known," she says—she took a job as a fact-checker and reporter at *Forbes* magazine, which enabled her to ask questions and learn about new worlds for a living. Next, she worked as a financial analyst on Wall Street, where she became curious about the emerging computer industry. This new interest eventually led her to acquire what she calls a "newsletter/conference boutique," which she renamed EDventure Holdings and uses as a perch from which to analyze the impact of emerging technologies and markets on society and business.

Dyson has many interests aside from information technology—"There's no *primary* one," she says—but two go all the way back to her youth. She first aimed to be a novelist and later expressed those literary aspirations in *Release 1.0*, EDventure's monthly newsletter, and her books *Release 2.0: A Design for Living in the Digital Age* and *Release 2.1*. Her other goal was to become a foreign correspondent in Moscow. She learned Russian in pursuit of that youthful dream, which helped her to make an adult one come true. In 2008 and 2009, Dyson spent six months in Russia earning certification as a cosmonaut.

Sounding like a physical as well as intellectual neophiliac, Dyson explains her desire for out-of-this-world adventure: "First of all, it's new. I always sit next to the window on airplanes, and space travel would be the ultimate looking-out-the-window experience. Second, I really like being weightless. When you're experiencing it, it doesn't feel amazing—it feels natural. You're not flying like a bird, which flaps and feels gravity, but floating. It feels like a return to a state of nature or grace, which is novel because we've been cut off from those experiences."

One night just after completing cosmonaut training, Dyson had a dream in which she was one of a group of kids floating in the air, keeping themselves in a weightless state just by thinking hard about it. When one boy forgot to concentrate, he flopped down harmlessly onto the floor, which made her laugh out loud and wake up. You don't have to be Sigmund Freud to see the connection between her dream and a high-flying life kept aloft by thinking very hard about new things.

All of us feel and function best when we achieve a balance between the need to be safe and the desire to be stimulated, which produces the ideal state called "optimum arousal." Too much exciting novelty and change, and you feel jittery or even panicky; not enough, and you're overcome with ennui. The level that's just right for you largely depends on your temperament, or your personality's more biological, heritable foundation.

# PART TWO

# Neophilia and You

*Four*

# You Meet New

IF YOU COULD spend a few moments watching a gang of the NIMH's monkeys cavorting in their playground, you'd soon identify the cautious neophobes, who peek at you from behind a barrier, and the outgoing neophiles and neophiliacs, who approach you in hopes of a treat, if the latter aren't too busy showing off or fighting. For that matter, if you've been acquainted with some skittish, extroverted, and feisty cats or dogs, you've experienced firsthand what the nascent fields of animal emotion and personality have documented: the tendency to either approach or avoid novelty is the most important stable behavioral difference among individuals in the same species, period.

Like our fellow creatures, we show big personal differences

in certain obvious and enduring attitudes toward newness and change, each of which has its own biological as well as behavioral signature. Even tiny infants express a preference for familiar or unfamiliar objects. Whether your own tendency in reacting to novelty is *approach, avoid, maybe,* or some variation on those themes, that temperamental inclination, which is about 50 percent heritable, will manifest in the things you do and the way you do them, from learning a skill to walking into a party of strangers.

Since Hippocrates, scientists have proposed many theories to explain our varying reactions to the new and different. Way back in the fifth century B.C.E., the father of medicine, who was also the first psychologist, developed an impressive personality "model," or simplified theoretical description, to explain our individual differences in behavior. The optimistic, energetic neophiles who want to approach novelty he called "sanguine." Fretful, moody neophobes were "melancholic." Irritable, impulsive neophiliacs were "choleric." His terminology is necessarily archaic, but these temperaments are as evident at a suburban mall as they were in the Athenian agora.

Hippocrates believed that we differ in quality, being either sanguine, say, or melancholic. However, modern psychologists assert that we vary quantitatively—that is, in terms of a small number of basic personality characteristics that all of us express in different degrees, from very little to a great deal. Partly for the practical reason that that's where most behavioral problems crop up, much of their research focuses on a trait's extremes, but by inference it also sheds light on more moderate expressions.

The field of personality psychology is notoriously disputatious, which is reflected in its different perspectives on the individual's affinity for the new and different. Some scientists regard neophilia as a hybrid trait arising from several more fundamental ones, while others maintain that it's a discrete temperamental characteristic in its own right. Some theories are based on subjects' observations of their own behavior, as elicited by questionnaires—Do you prefer variety or routine? Would you rather be in a storm at sea or visit a relative in the hospital for a week?—while others increasingly consider not only a person's behavior but also objective biological criteria, such as patterns of brain activity and neurochemical balances. To make matters still more complicated, various theorists give the trait their own spins and labels, including novelty, sensation, stimulation, and thrill seeking. Nevertheless, this large body of research offers important insights into human behavior in general and neophilia in particular.

If you're among the majority in the moderate middle, you express your affinity for novelty in countless everyday ways. Maybe you delight everyone at your office by figuring out how to do a boring job in a more interesting, efficient fashion. Perhaps you get hooked on travel cable TV shows and sign up for an exotic vacation. You decide to walk to work instead of taking the bus. You actually cook that recipe from the newspaper instead of just filing it away, and you even buy the ingredients in a different grocery store. You choose a film from Bollywood instead of Hollywood. You opt for a cutting-edge info gadget instead of sticking with the technology you already know. You surprise your beloved by refusing to play your usual role in your next fight. You start a book club.

Following your neophilia can lead to significant personal change and even a different way of life. Encouraged by his ESL teacher, a young blue-collar laborer decides to attend night school and becomes his family's first college graduate. A WASP lawyer broadens her horizons by learning Spanish and vacationing in South America instead of Southhampton. A battered wife gets help and leaves an abusive marriage. A small-town couple stuns their kids by retiring to a big city instead of a gated golf community.

Her healthy streak of neophilia gradually persuaded Kate Stone Lucas, born and raised in New York City, to take up a rural Western lifestyle. Her first step, made when she was a Dartmouth student, was to take a break from the East Coast preppy life and spend the summer working at a dude ranch southeast of Yellowstone National Park. The job, which involved both kitchen duties and handling horses, had a steep learning curve for a city slicker. Although she could ride, she had never sat on a Western saddle, much less backed up a stock trailer. Highlighting neophilia's raison d'être, she says, "I just learned how to do things as I went along."

Several ranch summers later, Lucas was about to head to Washington, D.C., and prepare to study law, but she paused to listen to her heart. Compared with those at neo-philia's extremes, who are primed to react instinctively to new things, the individuals in its broad moderate range have time to consider and modulate their responses. This behavioral flexibility, which allows them to be more selective about their experience, is one of their great strengths. After due reflection, says Lucas, "I realized I just couldn't go back East. Something in the West was calling to me."

Her family provided blessings but no funding for her pursuit of a new life, so Lucas scrimped to buy a hay field thirty miles out of town, moved into a camper on it, and took every job she could find, from bartending to cooking to giving riding lessons at the rodeo grounds. She found a spiritual home in a log-cabin church, learned Western swing dancing from a beau, and despite a certain natural reserve, delighted in many new friends, including a cowboy old enough to have known a guy who had worked for George Armstrong Custer. His primitive ranch was full of wild young horses that needed to be rounded up and gentled for sale as mounts, and he hired Lucas to do the hands-on work while he hollered tips from the porch. "You had to handle those horses with brooms till they were calm enough to touch," she says. "I got paid with one out of every three we sold."

After putting in seven hard years acquiring the wide range of skills that her new life required, Lucas inherited some money and took it to the next level by building the Whirling K equestrian center; its large indoor arena is a major asset for a horse-crazy community that contends with extreme weather. Running her business while caring for her husband and preschooler isn't always easy. The neophobes who are suspicious of novelty, prefer routine, and hew to traditional views are more numerous on islands and in America's middle and western states, so her progressive political and social ideas aren't universally popular in her conservative locale. Nevertheless, she has no regrets about the life she's created for herself: "There was no choice. I just didn't want to put on a suit and be like everyone else."

Now that the Whirling K is a dozen years old, Lucas is ready for the next adventure. Raising healthful, organic, grass-fed cattle is one possibility, she says, "because the ranching business is still fresh territory for me." Pondering the source of her urge to keep exploring and learning, she says, "It's not even a conscious thing, but something deep inside that says, 'It's time to try something new.'"

DIFFERENT PERSONALITY THEORIES use different language to express Lucas's neophilic attitude to novelty and change. The questionnaire-based "Big Five" model, for example, describes an individual's degree of engagement with the new in terms of two of its basic traits: extroversion, or outgoingness and liveliness, and the more intellectual, emotional quality called "openness to experience," which reflects curiosity, imagination, independence, insightfulness, creativity, and love of variety. (In one intriguing study, a larger-than-average hippocampus, a brain structure that helps you recognize, record, and recall new information, correlated with a strong expression of openness.) According to this scale, Lucas would be rated as moderate in extroversion and robust in openness. Although it has been criticized for the looseness of its definition and these fuzzy boundaries with the intellect, this felicitously named trait helps to counter the simplistic, stereotyped reduction of neophilia to hairy-chested physical risk taking and thrill seeking.

In a jargon-free discussion of the individuals who personify openness, psychologist Paul Silvia says, "They're quick to think, 'Hmm, my life is missing something. What can I do about that?'" Even if the solution involves a lot of uncertainty, as in "I don't know exactly how I'm going to manage to move to the West" or "start my own business," this fluid sense of identity appeals to them. In contrast, the neophobes, whom the Big Five scale describes as "closed to experience," have what he calls "a hard-edged sense of who they are and how life should be." They're inclined to think along the lines of "I am and will always be a well-paid data analyst/autoworker/executive at this company." When the traditional American middle-class narrative gets disrupted in times of social or economic turmoil, says Silvia, "that can really shake up such a person's identity."

If people comment on your home's unusual decor and large selection of books, music, and art, you might embody the strong connection between the trait of openness and creativity. In fact, the large body of research on the inventive personality in general adds an important scientific perspective on neophilia of the intellectual, emotional sort. First of all, the original thinker's *approach* response to new ideas and experiences correlates strongly with crystallized intelligence, or the acquired knowledge that's inspired by curiosity and interest. Creative work also requires good fluid intelligence—the capacity to reason quickly and think abstractly that's measured on standardized tests—but an IQ score of 120, which is twenty points above the average, is generally considered to be adequate.

Notwithstanding exceptions such as Freud and Goethe, genius-level intelligence can actually be an obstacle to inventiveness. A large study of children who had IQs of 180 and up suggests why. According to Mark Runco, a University of Georgia psychologist who studies creativity, most of these brilliant kids were unhappy campers who were "too obsessed with facts and correctness to cope with the ambiguous, messy real world." Bright as they were, they couldn't tolerate the uncertainties and frustrations inherent in doing something new and different and were better suited to logical, SAT-type pursuits. As if explaining the Peter principle, Oklahoma State University psychologist and creativity researcher Robert Sternberg says, "You see very smart people who aren't creative all the time. They do what they're told and are excellent analysts, so they're good on their first year on the job, but not so good when promoted."

The legendary bongo-playing physicist Richard Feynman, who had a fine if unremarkable IQ of 125, exemplified the creative personality's flexible, open attitude toward new experiences and ways of thinking. In addition to his Nobel Prize–winning contributions to science's understanding of the counterintuitive world of quantum physics, he was a passionate traveler, joker, artist, and samba *aficionado.* He married three times, experimented with psychedelic drugs, and sometimes saw the letters in black-printed equations in living color. It's no accident that his autobiographical books are called *Surely You're Joking, Mr. Feynman!* and *What Do You Care What Other People Think?,* and subtitled *Adventures of a Curious Character* and *Further Adventures of a Curious Character,* respectively.

As Feynman's titles suggest, intellectual novelty seekers must have the toughness and drive required to withstand the opposition, even ridicule, that new ideas often evoke. Feynman's intrinsic motivation was such that after releasing their labor-intensive research, his chagrined colleagues often found that he had reached the same conclusions long before but, unimpressed, simply hadn't bothered to publish his results. "These people set their own goals," says creativity researcher Dean Simonton. "Darwin really *wanted* to figure out where different species come from." Their rugged, uncensored, warts-and-all view of life, which causes them to notice many things, including negative ones, that others gloss over, is rooted in their relative lack of inhibition and repression. In his research on "remembered unhappiness," for example, the late Berkeley psychologist Donald MacKinnon found that most creative people have generally pleasant childhoods, but many recall them as having been less so. This original if unrosy perspective is exemplified by *The Simpsons*, whose fresh, offbeat humor derives from writer George Meyer's bittersweet recollections of his own childhood.

Finally, to the creative personality's recipe of good intelligence, robust neophilia, self-directedness, and the toughness that he describes as a low level of "harm avoidance," C. Robert Cloninger, a psychiatrist and neuroscientist at Washington University in Saint Louis who developed the Temperament and Character Inventory personality model, would add a big dollop of "reward dependence," or desire for approval. Rather than illustrating this persona with the usual attention-seeking if unconventional poet, painter, or diva, he shines the spotlight on actor-president Ronald Reagan, who was both creative in politics and personally engaging.

In his very different world, so, too, was the theatrical Feynman. A popular lecturer, he took special pride in distilling complicated physics to elegantly simple principles that he called "freshman explanations." Instead of giving the expert witness's usual windy technical analysis at the government's hearing on the space shuttle *Challenger*'s fatal explosion, the scientist, then dying of cancer, did a simple show-and-tell: He plunged one of the craft's O-ring seals into a glass of ice water, which made it stiffen, as had occurred on the disastrously cold day of the launch. Appropriately enough, this creative neophiliac's last words were, "I'd hate to die twice. It's so boring."

LARGELY THANKS TO technological advances in behavioral genetics, brain monitoring, and the like, biologically informed research on temperament increasingly provides the best insights into neophilia. Some of the keenest observations about the swashbuckling thrill seekers and sensitive souls at its extremes come from studies of the innate dispositions of boldness and shyness, which we all express to varying degrees. The adventurous yet socially reserved Lucas, for example, would fall into the higher mid-range of boldness and the mid-range of shyness. In his classic research on both traits, Harvard psychologist Jerome Kagan exposed infants and small children to mildly stressful forms of novelty—noise, sour tastes, unfamiliar objects or people—while he monitored their behavioral and physiological responses. He found that certain fearless tots, most of whom are boys, clearly warrant the label of "bold." Their physiological markers are a very low heart rate and a more active left brain.

Their active, spontaneous behavior and zestful, bring-it-on attitude toward new things bespeaks the instinctive energy and drive that Freud called "libido."

Story Musgrave, M.D., who's best known as the astronaut who repaired the Hubble telescope while floating in space some 370 miles above earth, expressed the neophiliac's strong bold streak very early on his family's thousand-acre New England farm. Describing himself as a "born explorer," he says, "I was in the forests alone at night at the age of three and on the rivers in my home-built rafts at five." By the time he turned ten, he was also operating and repairing tractors and other agricultural machinery—experience that would serve him well in his future career.

After dropping out of prep school, the restless young Musgrave joined the Marines and quickly fell in love with planes. In a textbook illustration of neophilia's purpose, this new interest led him to learn all sorts of skills, from flying to aviation mechanics. In time, he would put in nearly eighteen thousand hours in civilian and military aircraft as pilot, instructor, and acrobatics specialist. He would also make some six hundred parachute jumps, including free falls to study human aerodynamics. Supplying insight into the born thrill seeker's low-idling temperamental sangfroid, he says, "I'm a restless wanderer but in a calm, serene, and mindful way—certainly not agitated or frenetic."

After leaving the Marines, Musgrave focused on exploring new intellectual horizons. The high-school dropout eventually gathered postdoctoral degrees in mathematics, business administration, physiology, chemistry, literature, and computer science. For good measure, he also earned a doctorate in medicine from Columbia University and completed a surgical internship.

The NASA program, which began in 1958, might have been invented for intellectual and physical neophiliacs like Musgrave. The pilot-scientist-mechanic-surgeon was one of the first eleven people chosen from four thousand applicants. His thirty-year career with the agency lasted from the Apollo era of the 1960s to the space-shuttle program of the 1990s and involved everything from designing experiments to making five space walks.

Now retired from NASA, Musgrave takes deep satisfaction in the fact that his exploits have not only fulfilled his need for adventure but also contributed to the commonweal and inspired many young people. His personal goal has never been money or fame, he says, but simply "to live on the high ground of ultimate performance just for the sake of it, with no other gain." As to the drive that has led him to embody neophilia's high purpose of adapting to, learning about, and achieving new things, he says only that "there's an unquenchable restlessness and curiosity driven by some energy that pushes me forward. But the source . . . I don't have the answer for that."

An astronaut's uninhibited *approach* response to novelty exemplifies fearlessness, to be sure, but just as it falls short to describe Einstein as really good at physics or to give Shakespeare an *A* in English, the neophiliac's behavior is more than just a lack of anxiety. Such very bold individuals also respond more to reward than to punishment, for example, and even react less strongly to what anyone else would consider agony.

Indeed, when Musgrave describes undergoing a test of surviving extreme cold that tormented the NASA scientists who had
to monitor it, he says that what he experienced was "just pain."

In addition to boldness, neophiliacs are apt to have a
strong streak of Hippocrates' choleric disposition. This tendency to act first and ask questions later, which modern psychologists call "irritability" or "impulsivity," comes in handy
in the kind of high-octane situations that are familiar to Navy
Seals and others of that feisty ilk. In his primate populations,
psychologist Stephen Suomi, a temperament researcher at
the National Institute of Child Health & Human Development,
finds that the trait overlaps substantially with a readiness to
explore new environments, both social and physical. In short,
if boldness and cautiousness are what his former colleague
J. D. Higley, now a researcher at Brigham Young University,
wonderfully terms "the North and South of temperament,"
equanimity and this tendency to be easily riled and raring to
go are "its East and West."

MOST INDIVIDUALS AT neophilia's bold and cautious extremes
are born with a strong genetic push in those directions, yet
given the right experience, some people who begin life as shy
neophobes evolve into engaging neophiles. The new field of epigenetics, which examines how genes are expressed in the real
world, increasingly reveals the way in which nurture sculpts
your inborn disposition into the "second nature" that's the real
you, sometimes with surprising results. It's hard to imagine a
better example of such a transformation than Eleanor Roosevelt.

As a child, Eleanor would have fit right in with the most inhibited of Kagan's young research subjects. He found that when exposed to novel stimuli, the behavioral response of these temperamentally high-strung neophobes—often described by scientists as "sensitive" or "shy"—was avoidant, fearful, and inhibited. This group includes a sizable number of boys, but more are girls. They have a more active right brain, which is linked to anxiety and moodiness, and their heart rates and other measures of stress are higher than average. They're likelier to have blue eyes and narrow faces and to suffer from allergies and constipation. Just as their bold peers are explorative, these children are inclined to be thoughtful and reflective.

No one could possibly have imagined that the poor little rich girl who was so plain and shy that her socialite mother called her "Granny" would grow up not only to live in the White House but also to become what President Harry Truman called the "First Lady of the World." Orphaned at the age of ten and mostly raised by a grandmother, young Eleanor was described by her biographer Joseph Lash as insecure, starved for affection, and convinced of her ugliness.

Shy Eleanor's life began to change for the better at the age of fifteen, when a new experience pushed her from her natural neophobia toward a budding neophilia. Her relatives sent her to a rigorous finishing school in London that was run by a feminist educator who encouraged her students to be independent and think for themselves. She succeeded brilliantly with young Miss Roosevelt, who returned to New York with a notable increase in self-confidence and openness. Despite her status as a wealthy debutante, her new progressive convictions, combined with her innate sensitivity and compassion for others, led her to overcome her natural reserve and serve as a social worker in New York City's slums. Before long, she escorted her future husband and distant cousin, Franklin Delano Roosevelt, a dashing young Harvard neophiliac, on a tour of the pestilent tenements, which shocked and moved him.

Two major setbacks finally freed the courageous neophile from the chrysalis of Eleanor's earlier self. After Franklin was paralyzed in both legs by an illness assumed to be polio, her belief in their shared political ideals forced her to conquer her shyness to the point that she ably represented him in public. Giving speeches and shaking hands with strangers, she also became the essential conduit of the people's views to their handicapped leader.

After Franklin became president, a blow of a different kind pushed Eleanor to create a new private as well as public life. After discovering her spouse's first affair, she turned mostly to women for friendship and probably romance, which she often enjoyed in Franklin's gift of the Stone Cottage, her personal refuge on their Hyde Park estate. In addition, Eleanor had a very close relationship with her handsome, athletic male bodyguard, who taught her to enjoy sports and may also have been a lover.

In pursuing what became a highly adventurous life devoted primarily to securing human rights for the poor, minorities, women, and other have-nots—a wonderful positive expression of the shy temperament's sensitivity—the once timid little "Granny" mastered many roles, including politician, social activist, world traveler, author, speaker, and delegate to the

United Nations General Assembly. A famous *New Yorker* cartoon that sums up this remarkable self-made neophile shows a stunned coal miner deep in a dark tunnel looking up at a shining flashlight beam headed his way. The caption reads, "For gosh sakes, here comes Mrs. Roosevelt!"

JUST AS SOME temperament researchers would describe neophiliacs and neophobes as bold or shy, others would rate them according to their degree of novelty seeking or some variation on that term. Lying in a dark, soundproofed room for hours sounds like the very definition of boredom, but back in the 1960s, University of Delaware psychologist Marvin Zuckerman noticed something unusual about the volunteers for his sensory-deprivation experiments. Many of them were early countercultural types who had heard about his research and hoped that the sessions would provide them with kicks of the sort associated with psychedelic drugs. When he gave these free spirits some standard personality tests, he discovered that they shared a pronounced inclination toward novel, varied, complex, and intense experience. Intrigued, Zuckerman investigated further and identified a trait that he named sensation seeking. The foibles sometimes associated with its extremes notwithstanding, he says, "you might say that strong sensation seekers are more interesting people."

Sensation seeking isn't just about the quest for new experience but is also about the degree of emotional intensity, energy, and concentration—the *zeal*—with which it's pursued, whether in work or sports, relationships or the arts, driving style or food preferences. Even where its extreme's link with substance abuse is concerned, Zuckerman points out that the correlation lies more with the variety of drugs used than the type: "In a sense, these individuals are exploring their inner worlds and are willing to experiment to find novelty and arousal in the high."

All of us appear somewhere on the sensation-seeking continuum, and your reaction to the mere prospect of an intensely exciting activity—say, riding a world-class roller coaster—is enough to suggest your tendency. The neophobes on the low end of the scale get the willies just thinking about the stomach-fluttering experience. The neophiles in the middle range decide they'd try it once, if only to say they had. The neophiliacs at the continuum's high end, however, delight at the thought of the ride's intense arousal and anticipate lining up for repeat trips.

Strong sensation seekers have a cavalier attitude about any dangers associated with their exciting if not downright hair-raising pursuits. Even when they don't underestimate the risk involved, they're willing to proceed anyway, partly because they also anticipate greater rewards than others do. Just as Musgrave inevitably moved from parachute jumps to free falls, they'll soon adapt to a thrilling activity as its novelty wears off, prompting them either to come up with new and ever more exciting ways to do it or to switch to something else.

The whoopee-there's-a-roller-coaster aspect of sensation seeking, which Zuckerman calls "thrill- and adventure-seeking," is just the most obvious of the trait's four expressions, which all of us manifest in varying degrees. Many neophobes and moderate neophiles would measure highest in the more intellectual and emotional "experience-seeking." Others would be strongly susceptible to boredom, and still others to "disinhibition," or the orgiastic tendency to let it rip in company. Lucas expresses her affinity for the new and different most strongly in the higher moderate range of adventure and experience seeking, for example, while some full-tilt neophiliacs—Keith Richards springs to mind—would be off the charts in all four modes.

The question of how well the frisky contingent of *Homo sapiens* is coping with our increasingly sedentary, screen-oriented postindustrial world often invokes researchers' references to our necessarily adventurous evolutionary past. "Hunting large beasts is characteristic for males in our hominid species," says Zuckerman. "It's risky, but I'm sure the early hunters enjoyed it, as do remnants of the population still." The decline in opportunities to slay woolly mammoths and the like may help explain the increasing popularity of kill-it-and-grill-it survivalist TV shows such as *Man vs. Wild* and *Survivorman*, as well as risky, exciting activities like ice climbing and big-wave surfing. As Zuckerman says, "Sensation seekers who are bored by the modern workplace tend to look for thrills more in the off-hours, in things like extreme sports."

MANY IF NOT most psychologists now refer to our affinity for the new as "novelty seeking." In 1996, Cloninger and an international research team rocked the world of behavioral science by reporting the first empirical link between a gene and individual differences in behavior (to be discussed further in chapter 5). They found that strong novelty seekers are likelier than others to carry a variant of a gene that's unique to humans and affects dopamine's regulation in a way that inclines them toward what Cloninger calls "a distinctive pattern of reactivity and recovery." In short, they're quicker to be aroused by an exciting stimulus and also quicker to adapt to it and be primed for the next thrill.

Those who personify novelty-seeking's flared-nostril extreme are explorative, impulsive, irritable, extravagant, disorderly, and inclined toward overindulgence in food, alcohol, and drugs; what distinguishes their go-for-it response from a mere lack of inhibition is their strong *motivation* to pursue the different and exciting. By no means are all of them male CEO's, test pilots, or alpinists. A woman of this bold stripe might be an intensely sociable party animal who's easily bored and craves new experiences, friends, and lovers; she'd also be likely to gamble, say, and drive too fast, splurge, drink too much, and smoke. In contrast, the neophobes at the other end of the spectrum bring to mind the farmers in Grant Wood's *American Gothic*, being restrained, rigid, frugal, and stoic.

Novelty seeking is as characteristic of leaders as of big-wave surfers, and much depends on how an individual's temperamental inclinations are modified by his or her character. Borrowing from Immanuel Kant, Cloninger defines this quality as "what people make of themselves intentionally." In a neophile such as Lucas, for example, natural adventurousness is channeled in productive directions by the character traits that he calls self-directedness, cooperativeness, and self-transcendence. These strengths also continue to serve the neophiliac Musgrave since relinquishing space travel. He still flies, parachutes, scuba dives, lectures at the Kennedy Space Center and other venues, and writes scientific papers and poetry. He especially enjoys hanging out with his second wife and seven children, ages fifty to five years. "My little son Story is my hero," he says, "because he gets me to pursue *all* the opportunities and challenges that any life has to offer."

PERSONALITY RESEARCHERS MAY not agree on neophilia's precise recipe, much less on what to call it, but they speak with one voice about their most important practical finding: Whatever your characteristic response to the new, you need to understand and work with its inevitable pluses and minuses. Emily Dickinson's pained avoidance of novel stimuli was such that she confined herself to her home and yard, yet that same sensitivity inspired her exquisite poetry. As Cloninger puts it, "It's unlikely that any personality trait is 'good for you' per se. It's more that 'it's good for X behavior.' And the enhanced function in that niche will be balanced by some problem in another."

Some research on neophiliacs also illustrates the point. One study of eighty three- and four-year-olds found that the toughness that served the most fearless little novelty seekers so well in feats of playground derring-do could become a deficit in social interactions. These tots were sociable and friendly enough, but they were also often aggressive and lacking in empathy. They couldn't recognize when other kids were afraid, took advantage of friends, and weren't sorry when they behaved badly. In a complementary adult study, thrill-seeking fighter pilots were more conscientious, assertive, and fearless than other military flyers but also less agreeable. In other words, they were better suited to the cockpit than to the dinner party or PTA meeting.

It's not always easy to manage the ups and downs of one's own neophilia, but as Story Musgrove's adventurousness and Eleanor Roosevelt's sensitivity make plain, the larger population benefits from our variety. It's perhaps no accident that about the same 10 percent to 15 percent of Kagan's toddlers and Suomi's monkeys are either innately enthusiastic or anxious about the new and different in a broad range of situations and that the majority find more moderate ways to balance their desire for fresh experience with their need to feel safe. Whether it's liberals versus conservatives, risk takers versus the safety conscious, or technophiles versus technophobes, our conflicts can be uncomfortable, but ideally, the payoff of our different attitudes about novelty is a stronger, more resilient group as a whole.

It's hardly a coincidence that Zuckerman pioneered research on the behavior he calls sensation seeking. He later discovered that he carries the gene associated with the strong tendency, although he says that age has mellowed its influence: "My idea of sensation seeking now is riding on top of a double-decker bus on my sabbatical." Like his expression of neophilia, yours reflects the interaction between your experience and biology: genes, brain structures, and neurochemistry, particularly the important transmitter dopamine.

*Five*

# The Alchemy of
# Anticipation

Y OUR PERSONAL EXPRESSION of neophilia is rooted in your brain's particular chemistry and anatomy. When you encounter something new, the two systems collaborate in producing your general level of arousal and the ratio between your fear of risk and hope of reward, which in turn motivates your emotional response, be it *approach, avoid,* or *maybe.* Their respective roles are hard to tease apart, but a single burst of a neurotransmitter or hormone can affect many brain parts, which gives chemistry a broader impact than any one structure.

Neophilia's elixir is dopamine. Like other neurotransmitters, it passes electrochemical messages from one neuron across a synapse, or gap, to receptor sites on another in a lock-and-key fashion. Dopamine is involved in practically everything you do, from physical movement (a deficiency causes Parkinsonism) to learning, but it's especially important to neophilia's behavioral building blocks: motivation, anticipation, and the seeking and processing of both novelty and rewards. Thus, our individual dopamine profiles go a long way toward explaining our different responses to the new and exciting.

Dopamine makes you want things, especially new or pleasurable ones. Whenever you encounter something that's enjoyable, like a glass of wine, or intriguingly novel, like a glamorous stranger at a neighborhood party, a spritz of dopamine jacks up your level of arousal, focuses you on that target, and mobilizes your explorative *approach* response—a symphonic collaboration that you experience as "Go for it!"

The strong association between the new and the enjoyable, right down to those ill-advised shopping sprees and dubious assignations, helps account for neophilia. Not all rewards are novel, nor are all pleasures new, but they often overlap. Moreover, we'll work hard for both. That's not surprising where rewards are concerned, but even well-nourished animals can get cabin fever in their comfy lairs and head outside just for a change of scene. Explaining why so many explorers willingly undergo excruciating torments on their quests, Robert Falcon Scott (who died of starvation and exposure while returning from the South Pole) put it this way: "Every day some new fact comes to light—some new obstacle which threatens the gravest obstruction. I suppose this is the reason which makes the game so well worth playing." Underscoring this connection between the new and the pleasurable, Vanderbilt University neuroscientist David Zald says, "Passionate surfers and skiers claim that the wave or the slope is never exactly the same. There's always that sense of newness and exploration."

Novelty and reward aren't necessarily the same, but one thing they *do* have in common is dopamine and its tonic effect on your motivation to pursue a goal—whether it's something new or something enjoyable. For a long time, the transmitter was regarded as what University of Michigan neuroscientist Kent Berridge calls "the common neurocurrency of all pleasant things." In an important recent breakthrough, however, scientists discovered that the dopamine system sometimes reacts to a reward and sometimes doesn't, but it *always* responds to cues that predict one. In other words, dopamine has more to do with the anticipation and pursuit of the new and/or rewarding than the actual savoring of it. As Berridge neatly puts it, "Dopamine is about wanting rather than liking."

As you know if you've ever disgusted yourself by wolfing down a second piece of pie even though you felt full, *wanting*—the anticipatory craving for something that's often but not always needed—and *liking*—the actual feeling of pleasure and enjoyment that it provides—can occur independently. Animal research suggests dopamine's role in each sensation. When the transmitter's balance is artificially depleted in certain rats, for example, their desire for food is reduced but not their satisfaction if they're force-fed. In contrast, mice whose dopamine balances have been deliberately hiked up show greater *wanting* but not *liking* of sweets.

Like dopamine, neophilia is all about anticipation, desire, *wanting*. The transmitter contributes to the behavior by etching into your brain a learned link between novelty and reward, which motivates you to pursue the former to attain the latter. Exhibit A is the astoundingly popular phenomenon of video gaming. About seventy million Americans already indulge, and the average young person devotes ten thousand hours to the activity before turning twenty-one.

Game designers are experts in generating a drug-free neophiliac high based on deluging you with exciting new challenges and short-term rewards for your progress as you figure them out. This constant stream of novel stimuli and small bonuses keeps triggering the release of dopamine, which generates more *wanting,* which in turn motivates you to keep going—and going—for the ultimate jackpot. This seductive dynamic explains why gaming can become an obsession that causes some players to neglect school, work, relationships, and even sleep to the point of collapsing from exhaustion.

Of course, the way in which dopamine can encode an anticipation of reward into your brain can also reinforce positive behavior, from the explorer's quest to the mastery of a new sport. Educators interested in using gaming technology in the classroom speculate that the same combination of exciting novelty and frequent rewards that enthralls kids with Epic Mickey could keep them engaged in math and history. That's not such a far-fetched idea. The military already uses Space Fortress and America's Army to train pilots and recruits, and intelligent games such as SimCity 2000 and Rise of Nations were specially designed to encourage original thinking, good problem solving, and sound decision making.

Speaking of decisions, dopamine's urgent whispers about wonderful rewards that await you just ahead can sometimes have an unfortunate, even disastrous impact on the choices you make in exciting situations. Duke University's behavioral economist Dan Ariely found a serious gap between what male undergraduates say about safe sex, for example, when they're cool, calm, and collected and what they actually do in the dopamine-drenched heat of the moment. It's not a calamity if the transmitter whets your appetite for a fattening pastry as you walk past the bakery. If the prospect of making a killing in the stock market activates dopamine's pedal-to-the-metal circuitry, however, you could end up in the poorhouse.


NO MATTER WHERE you're situated on neophilia's spectrum, there are good reasons for knowing something about the biological as well as behavioral profiles of its extremes. First, there's up to a 30 percent chance that you belong to one of them. Even if you don't, there's almost a 100 percent chance that you know or are even related to someone who does. A little understanding of neophiliac neurophysiology also adds to the portraits of many historical figures responsible for some of *Homo sapiens*'s greatest achievements. We don't know anything about the explorers who led our great migrations from Africa as individuals, but the biographies of their successors provide insights into what they must have been like. One homegrown example is Christopher Houston Carson, aka Kit (1809–68), who was America's first pop action hero.

Raised on the frontier of Boone's Lick, Missouri, Carson dropped out of school at the age of nine to hunt and help support his large family. At sixteen, he ran off to the truly wild West, settled in Taos, New Mexico, and set about creating a life that vividly illustrates how neophilia enhances survival by helping us to adapt to and learn new things. To live in a radically different world that few people, Native American or white, had ever seen, young Carson acquired the mountain man's skills of the trapper, gunsmith, tailor, blacksmith, angler, climber, canoeist, miner, and cook (his rugged circle's favorite dish was beaver tail). Although illiterate, he learned fluent Spanish and several tribal languages and also became an acknowledged expert in negotiating with as well as fighting Indians.

Of all his talents, however, Carson was most famed as a tracker and explorer—perhaps the quintessential neophiliac vocation. After their accidental meeting, he joined John Charles Frémont, an army officer and topographer, in the quest to map much of the West, including the Oregon Trail, Mexican-controlled California, the central Rockies, and the Great Basin. Historical accounts particularly remark his lightning-quick arousal at new stimuli, whether a wolf pack or an Indian ambush, and almost instant adaptation, which enabled him to take action calmly while others stood slack jawed and white knuckled. Based on contemporaries' observations, one biographer described him this way: "Kit waited for nobody."

Carson's adventures certainly brought him plenty of the thrills that neophiliacs crave, but they also greatly advanced the interests of a young, expanding America and paved the way for the pioneers' great Western migration. The stagey Frémont was acclaimed as "the Pathfinder," but in his own lifetime, Carson was apotheosized in some twenty-five "dime novels" as a buckskin-clad demigod who helped to set the standard for America's eager approach to new frontiers of all kinds, from territory to technology to the arts.

We don't have Carson's genetic profile, of course, but this neophiliac's peripatetic behavior and high-speed arousal-adaptation response to the new suggest that he could well have carried a normal, nonpathological variant, or allele, of a dopamine receptor gene called DRD4, which receives signals from dopaminergic cells that fire in response to new stimuli and rewards. The most definitive research concerns the gene's slightly longer 7R version. To make a long, complicated story short, this allele produces a nervous system that has what scientists call a "low affinity" for dopamine and a temperament associated with hyperexcitability, strong novelty and reward seeking, and a tendency to adapt to arousing experiences fast and thus be ready for more. (For additional information, please see *Notes.*) Of DRD4's alleles, 7R has the lowest affinity for dopamine and the greatest impact on behavior, followed in descending order by 5R and 2R. These genetic factors help to explain some but by no means all extreme novelty seeking, as well as to illuminate the complex interactions of nature and nurture, and the subtle way in which biology can influence our thoughts, feelings, and actions.

According to one neuroscientific scenario, when individuals who have a naturally turbocharged dopamine system encounter something new or potentially pleasurable, they experience what Zald calls a "double whammy." The initial burst of the transmitter floods their already revved-up circuitry, causing a rush that motivates still more novelty or reward seeking. This dynamic, which he describes as "almost a reinforcement or a chain of events that feeds on itself," can keep these individuals perpetually treadmilling toward the next new thrill or high. Instead of and sometimes in addition to drugs, neophiliacs adjust their dopamine levels with exciting experiences. As Zald says, "Our lab thinks that a person who finds novelty and excitement more engaging does so because those things give him more dopamine release—more of a boost."

SOME OF THE most fascinating insights into genes, dopamine, and neophilia come from research on attention-deficit/hyperactivity disorder. People diagnosed with ADHD and 7R carriers are both apt to have the same low affinity for the transmitter, which is ameliorated by both Ritalin and thrills. Like neophiliacs, wiggly ADHD kids are subject to boredom, which could be relieved by exciting experiences as well as stimulants that raise their level of arousal. In fact, one reason why both groups are likelier to smoke and use drugs may be that they're self-medicating not so much for a high as just to feel better or "normal."

Like fever, ADHD can have many causes. Robert Moyzis, a molecular geneticist at UC Irvine, and his colleague James Swanson, a psychologist who's an expert on attention problems, discovered that the disorder's well-known association with the DRD4 gene is primarily explained by its 7R allele. Moreover, their research persuades them to dispute the assumption that the restless behavior linked to the disorder is necessarily problematic, even in our tame postindustrial settings. The children in their ADHD study who carried 7R were hyper and impulsive for sure, but they had none of the neurological or cognitive impairments that many of the other kids so diagnosed had. In fact, despite being the proverbial handful, these bright, enterprising youngsters struck the researchers as "superkids." Once they either matured into better self-control or transferred to more compatible schools, they performed well academically.

These smart, antsy 7R kids illustrate the complex way in which biology can influence seemingly "psychological" behavior such as distractedness and thrill seeking. The neurons in the prefrontal cortex and other areas that are most affected by the allele are so-called inhibitory nerve cells. Somehow, 7R eases the brakes on these neurons where both movement and attention are concerned. Thus, carriers have more trouble staying still and focused, particularly in constrained settings. However, like the illiterate Carson—and the many pro athletes who were "too cool for school" and struggled through college—they also have a much faster reaction time than others. "These individuals operate at a little more of a hair trigger," says Moyzis. "That's why 7R kids are always jumping around."

To illustrate how a physiological trait can shape a whole personality, Moyzis conjures up the image of a peppy 7R third-grader who's a daredevil on the playground. He has a genuinely better reaction time than the other kids, so he cuts capers that many of his friends and elders consider risky because they can't do such things. "But in fact," says Moyzis, "he *can*." Observing that downhill skiers have a higher frequency of the 7R allele, he says, "We gravitate toward things that we can do and enjoy. So maybe it's not entirely 'This is how your brain was hardwired, so this is how you behave.' Maybe it's subtler, as in 'People with faster reactions are drawn to different activities than those with slower reactions.'"

Our postindustrial culture, which rewards people who are suited to spending long hours staring at data on glowing screens, may look askance at neophiliacs in the schoolroom and office, but adventurous, explorative behavior can be highly adaptive, particularly in fluid situations. As Moyzis says, "In our early African days and as we moved into new environments worldwide, a lot of big creatures were trying to eat us. Being very focused probably wasn't a good thing at that time, because you had to constantly scan your environment in order to survive." Even in the constrained environment of a high-tech workplace, someone who's naturally inclined to scan the surroundings for incoming information may be less frustrated by constant distractions from various electronic media than his or her focused colleagues.

Paraphrasing the flood of feedback that his team's research elicits from relieved parents of 7R children who've been diagnosed with ADHD, Moyzis says: "Wait a minute! This puts things in a new perspective. At one point in human history, this was a very good gene to have! I *knew* there wasn't really anything wrong with my kid. It's just that his energy level is higher, or he's bored in school." Highlighting the fact that many neophiliacs lead successful lives—and that there's more to life than crunching data at a desk—he adds that "you wouldn't believe the amount of mail I get from people, particularly Californian entrepreneurial types, who say that they hated school and were diagnosed with ADHD, but now they're successful innovators."

Interestingly, 7R seems to confer a big advantage at the other end of the age spectrum. When Moyzis analyzed data from an in-depth, thirty-year-long study of the medical records of a large elderly population, he found that the individuals who carried the allele lived longer and were much likelier to be active well into old age, playing tennis, say, or hiking into their eighties and even nineties. Moreover, he discovered an important practical demonstration of epigenetics: The 7R subjects who kept fit and exercised did not develop Alzheimer's disease, while those who had the allele but not the discipline had the same incidence as the general population. Everyone knows that exercise is good for you, but perhaps 7R is, too, because it can motivate you to be the kind of person who exercises.

ALONG WITH NEUROCHEMICAL and genetic research, neuroanatomical studies, advanced by sophisticated scanning technology, have greatly enhanced the understanding of neophilia's biology by revealing what goes on in your brain when you encounter something new. Processing novelty involves an array of structures. (For additional information, please see *Notes*.) However, the amygdala, which invests stimuli with emotional meaning, has emerged as what Jane Joseph, a neuroscientist at the Medical University of South Carolina, calls the "big player." This touchy structure was long regarded as the brain's major threat detector, but recent research shows that the amygdala responds to anything, good or bad, that you consider salient, or important, from a stripper to a snake—and especially to novelty and change.

Interestingly, the brains of neophiliacs and neophobes react to new things differently in both sequence and intensity. When thrill seekers spot a raccoon in the backyard, say, or a pitcher of margaritas at a party, they first experience an active *approach* reaction that springs from the swift activation of the insula, a structure that helps govern visceral and emotional arousal. Instantly, they're excited by the new stimulus and ready to engage with it. The judgmental anterior cingulate cortex, which helps to dampen iffy behavior, only kicks in after they're already primed to proceed. Neophobes' brains react to the wild raccoon or the mind-bending cocktails in the opposite way. As if their nervous systems were protecting them from too much excitement, their initial *avoid* response originates in the cautious anterior cingulate cortex, while the fire-your-jets insula stays quiet.

Research on sensation seeking shows the same neophiliac pattern of intense, speedy arousal and quick adaptation to exciting new things. When subjects listen to a series of tones, the strong sensation seekers have a greater response to the first new sound than others, as measured by changes in their heart rate and galvanic skin response. When the audio series is repeated, however, they also get used to it much more quickly than the others do. Translating this physiological response into behavioral language, personality theorist Marvin Zuckerman says, "They pursue novelty because they get a kick out of it, but their rapid habituation means that they continually need fresh ways to get that kick."

Summarizing a lot of neuroscience, Joseph says that compared with neophiliacs, neophobes "would be quicker to think, 'Oops, I can't respond to that erotic stimulus because I'm at a business meeting.'" (For additional information, please see *Notes.*)

These innate differences in how our brains process new things and adapt to arousal help explain many a couple's arguments about subjects from flirtatiousness to how fast to drive to what to do on vacation. Stressing the practical importance of the fact that what you complacently think of as objective reality is far more subjective and fragmented than you assume, Joseph says. "The same new stimulus can tweak different nervous systems very differently, so that someone else may just chuckle at what you see as frightening."

As GALILEO AND Jackson Pollock knew, coping with wild, confusing new concepts that conflict with the world as you and everyone else have known it can be as difficult as taking on risky physical challenges. Where intellectual neophilia is concerned, scanning studies reveal that the brain of a Wynton Marsalis wrestling with a new composition or a Zaha Hadid designing a new building shows distinctive patterns of neurological activity. Simplistic pop theories about the roles of the "creative" right brain versus the "analytical" left brain have been oversold, and both are engaged in innovative work. However, thinking in a very specific, targeted way particularly activates the left temporal and frontal lobes, where facts and specifics are housed and processed. Pondering of a broader, more open-ended sort especially excites the right temporal and frontal lobes, which increases your chances of finding new ideas and associations among concepts.

Striking the ideal balance between narrowly targeted, fact-oriented thinking and the wide-angled, free-ranging, original sort is vital to your efficient functioning in general and creative work in particular. "If you process information at the maximum level of coarseness, everything is linked, which is useless," says Oshin Vartanian, a psychologist at Defense Research and Development Canada–Toronto who studies creativity and problem solving. "But if you process information at a maximum level of fineness, nothing will be linked. The trick is finding the right level of specificity for the task at hand, which for creative activities will probably require right frontal lobe activity."

Einstein's ability to interpret the same old math and science that his peers knew by heart in bold new ways testifies to his virtuosity in this neophilic, uninhibited, right-brain thinking. If you were asked to come up with several inventive solutions to a problem while under a sophisticated brain scanner, it's likely that the images would show that your right ventro-lateral prefrontal cortex had ramped up to jump-start original thinking. This activation would ease your apprehensiveness about novel ideas and help you to loosen up, go with the flow, lose yourself in your task, and see fresh possibilities. Combined with older personality and behavioral studies, such recent neuroscience supports the thesis that disinhibition, or letting go, is a key underlying mechanism of creativity and intellectual neophilia. As Vartanian says, "Novelty seeking is talked about as if there's a new object out there somewhere that you find, but usually it's the perceiver who has to interpret it as novel. Creative people can see things in a fresh way and produce new ideas because they can relax the usual perceptual and conceptual constraints that define entities."

Consider a difficult question that needs some original thinking: What is the nature of consciousness? If you take the conventional analytical, problem-solving route, you'll zero right in on the issue and try to get to the bottom of it. You'll employ "convergent" thinking, which processes well-defined, rational questions that have one solution, such as $1 + 1 = 2$, and is measured by standardized tests like the SAT. You'll make a list of things to consider, analyze the relevant information, and attempt to figure out the problem like a puzzle. (Interestingly, autistic "savants" use this strict problem-solving approach, but despite their prodigious abilities in specific domains, such as drawing, music, and math, they rarely make something utterly new.) You'll try this and that, but before long, the problem's complexity and many unknowns, combined with your fear of wasting valuable time, will elicit a strong *avoid* reaction, and you'll give up.

A creative, neophilic *approach* response to this tough problem involves a very different, "divergent" way of thinking. You recognize that an issue as complicated as consciousness resists direct analytic attack, so you allow your mind to relax. You chew on the subject for a while, wondering about some related questions. Is consciousness a matter of mind or of brain? Executive control? Subjective awareness, à la Descartes' *Cogito ergo sum*? Or Heidegger's *Dasein,* "being there"? Perhaps you read some John Locke and Antonio Damasio. Then you go for a walk or even work on another project for a spell—activities that could illuminate your problem from a new angle and point you toward a potential solution.

As you follow your neophilia down this winding road, you may solve the mystery of consciousness. Even if you don't, however, you'll learn a lot of new things, get some good insights that otherwise wouldn't have come your way, and perhaps find another, more accessible problem. As Vartanian puts it, "Creativity involves the knack of knowing when the specificity of a problem space is too high, then stepping away from it. Reducing the constraints allows seemingly unrelated new things to come to mind, which increases your chances of success."

Science has so far revealed more about original thinking's neuroanatomy than its neurochemistry. However, Robert Cloninger points to evidence that creative efforts such as musical improvisation—and interestingly, giving to charities—activate the brain's dopaminergic reward centers. Zald observes that a burst of dopamine could help launch a "flight or jump of new ideas." After all, such cognitive and emotional surges are characteristic not only of creative work but also of the high produced by drugs that affect the dopamine system, such as cocaine and amphetamine. Citing a brilliantly inventive entertainer as an example, he says, "Robin Williams was funniest of all when he was on coke. The audience had to struggle to keep up with his amazing leaps of thought."

MOST OF THE biological integers of your distinctive reaction to the new and different are hidden from the naked eye, but not all. Anyone who has ever been a teenager, let alone raised one, knows that the tendency to experiment with new things, chase thrills, and take risks peaks in adolescence, then gradually declines with the years. "Novelty seeking is a highly important aspect of adolescence—an area of expertise for teenagers," says NIMH psychiatrist and neuroscientist Daniel Pine. "We see the same thing in other young mammals, which suggests that it's part of the universal mammalian experience of having to leave the family structure at that age."

Even Keith Richards has slowed down with the years, and by the time you reach your sixties, your urge to experiment and take risks typically falls to half of what it was in high-spirited adolescence. This more temperate behavior is usually attributed to the accumulation of learning and wisdom, but biological changes wrought by time, such as shifts in the levels of hormones and other neurochemicals, are as likely a cause. "We explore new things less as we age, and we're also less able to adapt to them," says Zald. "My dad is a brilliant guy—a retired professor who still writes scholarly articles—but if you start to show him how to do something new on his computer, he's like *aargh!* It's too much."

Like age, gender is a visible biological difference that can affect neophilia's expression, but its effects aren't as easily categorized as you might think. For that matter, Cloninger finds that when comparing men's and women's personality profiles, the only broad difference in traits is women's greater sociability and cooperativeness. Pine's study of teenage boys and girls who had problems with meeting and greeting strangers—a form of novelty that's particularly important for sociable *Homo sapiens,* especially adolescents—offers neuroscientific support for this gender difference. The shy teens were asked to look at photos of unfamiliar peers, then to rate their potential as future online friends. The mere prospect of an interaction with strangers sent the girls' brains into a state of high arousal, which suggests a hypersensitivity to novel social encounters. The boys' brains didn't react in this agitated way, which confirms the conventional wisdom about Venus and Mars.

Compared with women, men have higher levels of testosterone and lower levels of an enzyme called monoamine oxidase A—a balance that when pronounced is particularly associated with the neophiliac's mad, wild excesses. Such neurochemical differences between the sexes could help explain why some studies show that female novelty lovers are likelier to pursue unconventional hobbies, interests, travel, and lifestyles than to go in for risky, thrill-seeking physical activities such as exploring or big-game hunting. Nevertheless, there have always been women who managed to do all of the above.

An unsung nineteenth-century contemporary of Kit Carson's, Lucy Ann Lobdell was born in rural Long Eddy, New York, and was already famed as a wildlife stalker and marksman in her teens. In short order, she married, gave birth, and was deserted by her abusive husband. Leaving her child with her parents, she adopted male dress and spent the next eight years living in and on the wilds. When an illness forced her to return home, she wrote an account of her adventures, including the bagging of 168 deer, 77 bears, and 1 panther.

After regaining her strength, Lobdell again found civilization too constraining. She donned male garb once more, styled herself Joseph Lobdell, and supported herself as an itinerant music teacher. She even won the heart of a socially prominent maiden but was forced to flee before their marriage when her gender was discovered. When a second health crisis sent her to the poorhouse, she wooed another young woman, and the pair took to the road as the Reverend Joseph Lobdell and wife. They lived mostly in the wilds and subsisted on what Lobdell could shoot or forage, but they made occasional appearances in public with a bear they had tamed. Eventually, perhaps because the stress of maintaining her highly novel way of life in a staid Victorian society helped to push Lobdell beyond her limits, she died in a mental asylum. The only clear diagnosis is that this physical, emotional, and social neophiliac lived a remarkable life at least a century too soon.

Biology may lay down neophilia's foundation, but your life experience plays a powerful role in forming your personal response to the new and different. That's why Zald gives the following advice to parents who are worried about how best to raise their neophiliac progeny: "Try to direct that tendency in a positive direction. Let them learn rock climbing but insist they do it in a club, so they get the excitement but within some constraints."

*Six*

# Novelty and Nurture

Both your genes and environment affect your behavior, but it's increasingly clear that what most matters is the interaction between them. This collaboration is especially apparent in childhood, but as the development of character, creativity, and other capacities show, the phenomenon of epigenetics persists throughout life and can be cultivated to your advantage. Moreover, just as experience can modulate an individual's temperamental response to newness and change, culture can manipulate a society's expression of neophilia by influencing the population's genetic balance.

Animal studies that for ethical reasons can't be done with human beings offer powerful insights into how genes and environment forge an individual's characteristic response to new things. Some of the most interesting research concerns the primates known as "weed species." As this tag suggests, these resilient, ubiquitous creatures are distinguished by their remarkable abilities to adapt to different situations, which enables them to thrive far from their original habitats.

Like us, rhesus and capuchin monkeys are notable for the fact that you can find them anywhere. Native to India, rhesus flourish in hot, humid tropical forests and the cold, dry Himalayas, in isolated wildernesses and densely populated megacities. South America's capuchins similarly prosper in the steamy Amazon basin and the icy Andes. "Move them to a new place," says temperament researcher Stephen Suomi, "and somebody in the group will figure out how to survive."

Much of the weed species' success at adapting to the unfamiliar springs from their rich genetic diversity. Like ours, rhesus groups include carriers of genetic variants that mediate major neurotransmitters such as dopamine and serotonin and thus their emotional responses to the world. (Suomi has yet to test capuchins but believes they're similar in this regard.) These hereditary differences create a lot of behavioral ones within a particular troop, from the neophiliacs' fearless exploration of the unknown to the neophobes' caution about it. All of this variety in turn makes the population flexible as a whole and able to adjust to a wide range of settings. Groups of other primates that are closely related to the protean weed species, such as the great apes, lack these genetic variations, so they can't just pick up and live in any old place, says Suomi: "Their home environments are actually quite restricted."

Despite these two weed species' probable genetic similarities, however, rhesus and capuchins have very different strategies for adapting to the unfamiliar that derive from their early social experiences. Like human beings and other Old World monkeys, rhesus form very tight mother-infant bonds. The members of their big, noisy, up-close-and-personal groups naturally band together to exploit new environments and scare off predators.

The social lives of the New World capuchins offer a chilly contrast. Their babies don't become very attached to their mothers. Their troops are much smaller, and individuals spend only a third as much time grooming one another and playing or fighting. These independent soloists adapt to new places not through cooperative action and fellow feeling but through individual diligence and hard work. Instead of monkeying around together, capuchin individuals spend two thirds of the day exploring, experimenting, and making special tools to get hard-to-access food.

In sum, both of these primate weed species are well suited by nature to deal with novelty. Their very different nurture, however, inclines capuchins to adapt to new territory like the autonomous, resourceful mountain men, while the rhesus resemble the West-bound pioneer families who circled their wagons each night.

Far from wild habitats, primate research conducted in controlled settings underscores how profoundly environmental influences can shape not only a group's responsiveness to the new and different but also an individual's. Stressing the importance of what psychologists call the person-environment fit, Suomi says that novelty seeking is "sometimes highly adaptive and sometimes not. When you're in an unpredictable, potentially dangerous setting, the tendency to explore and push the envelope can either find you a route to survival or get you killed. If you live in a very stable, unchanging setting, too much of that can get you into trouble. It depends on the circumstances."

Experiments with genetically fearful or bold infant monkeys that are raised by foster mothers with contrasting dispositions and various parenting skills provide important insights into the interactions between heredity and environment that affect neophilia's expression. Experience's impact is clearest in the individuals at the behavior's shy, timid extreme. These natural neophobes, whom Suomi calls "uptight," are inherently more sensitive, "so they'll suffer more than average if their environment isn't supportive. In a stable situation where stuff is basically provided, so they don't have to go out and get it, they'll also benefit more. Given an encouraging mother, such a youngster will develop quite well."

The environment's formative influence is less predictable where little neophiliacs are concerned. By and large, these naturally bold babies, described by Suomi as "laid back," are less affected by the quality of nurture they receive, whether good or bad. Their active dopamine systems help prime them for exploring new social and physical settings, taking chances, and acting impetuously. Many of them duly mature into fear-less thrill seekers, yet others don't. Some suffer no ill effects from being reared by a poor mother in a subpar environ-ment, but others get into the habit of doing impulsive, stupid things. Certain simian neophiliacs even develop behavioral problems when they're placed with a skilled foster mother in a seemingly optimum environment. As Suomi says, "It's too boring for them, so they get into trouble."

Animal research shows that given good nurture, even many young neophiliacs, and especially neophobes whose genes put them at risk for different behavioral problems, will turn out to be normal or better than normal. Where human beings are concerned, some of the best insights into the interactions of heredity and the context in which it's expressed come from the careful, long-term studies conducted by University of Helsinki psychologist Liisa Keltikangas-Järvinen and her col-leagues. She finds that children who carry alleles that produce a low affinity for dopamine and thus behavioral excitability—in Finland and northern Europe, mostly DRD4's 2R and 5R variants—are much likelier to become extreme novelty seek-ers *if* they are raised in certain kinds of environments. In the Finnish studies, genetically predisposed children who also had emotionally distant, strict mothers were significantly more inclined to develop neophiliac behavior than such children reared in more supportive homes. Nor was the domestic set-ting's emotional atmosphere the only environmental factor that could influence the trait's expression in the genetically inclined. High maternal education, household income, and paternal alcohol consumption, as well as an urban residence, also increased the likelihood of developing neophiliac tendencies. Based on her findings, Keltikangas-Järvinen concludes that "sensitivity to environmental adversities and benefits may be conditional on genetic background, and the nature-nurture interactions may be of greater importance than direct gene-trait associations." Indeed, she says, "it seems highly plausible that the effects of genes may become evident only when studied in the context of environmental factors."

Personality psychologists often say that the only difference between thrill-seeking cops and robbers is their different upbringings. No one would dispute the importance of early home life, but it's not the only environmental influence on the expression of an individual's temperament and his or her character development. As a teenager, Story Musgrave, who grew up in a troubled family, found the structure and support he needed from the Marines, which set him on a hero's path. Similarly, although he had been an oppositional child who was impervious to discipline, a neophiliac research subject studied by the late personality psychologist David Lykken eventually encountered a teacher whom he really admired and respected. The boy didn't want to disappoint this new mentor with bad behavior, so he decided to channel his choleric, thrill-seeking nature into socially acceptable realms. He grew up to lead a successful life that included guiding expeditions to the earth's wild places, but he always stressed that without that teacher's influence, he could have easily become a criminal instead of an adventurer.

Research often focuses on the darker dimensions of human behavior, but a particularly inventive study of gene-environment interaction involving two thousand subjects looked at their politics instead of their problems. Our red-state-versus-blue-state divisions, like many regional conflicts around the world, make plain that ideologies are influenced by social contexts. However, as research on the strongly heritable, rigid, judgmental, tradition-minded personality sometimes described as "authoritarian" has long suggested, such viewpoints can also have a genetic component. In an experiment that highlights evolution's way of ensuring different attitudes toward novelty and change, James Fowler, who's a professor of both genetics and political science at UC San Diego, found that young people who carry the 7R allele tend to become liberals rather than conservatives—but only if, as was the case for that notable neophiliac Bill Clinton, their adolescence featured many friends and exposure to multiple points of view. If either the gene or the active social life was missing, this ideological effect disappeared. As Fowler says, "This research highlights the importance of incorporating both nature and nurture into the study of political preferences."

In sum, human and animal studies show that like your other behaviors, your characteristic response to novelty and change develops from the interactions of your genes with your environment and with one another. Genes affect body type, for example, and a bold, athletic mesomorph who grows up outdoors, as Musgrave, Kit Carson, and Lucy Lobdell did, is likely to gravitate to the vigorous, adventurous activities that will reinforce a thrill-seeking disposition. Moreover, no trait exists in a vacuum but affects and is affected by your other characteristics. Thus, a neophiliac who lacks directedness and self-control is a very different person from one who is purposeful and able to govern his or her impulses. Indeed, as Robert Cloninger points out, robust novelty seeking is strongly correlated with antisocial behavior only in those individuals who also have serious character flaws or personality disorders, such as psychopathy. Where our behavioral patterns are concerned, says Suomi, "innate disposition helps, but experience can push that around quite a bit, in both positive and negative directions."

NURTURE'S EARLY IMPACT on nature is important, but some cutting-edge neuroscience from the other end of the chronological spectrum shows that novel experience can improve your mental and physical health well into old age. The least common denominator in the rejuvenating regimens that beef up brain and body is stepping up to a challenge, which by definition involves something new or different: beginning a daily walking program or training for a marathon, joining a choir or writing a musical.

Not long ago, scientists would have pooh-poohed the idea that by continuing to test their mental and physical mettle, seventy- and eighty-year-olds could build up their brains, improve their functioning, and reduce their risk of Alzheimer's disease. "My colleagues would have said, 'No way! It's all downhill from there," says Art Kramer, a cognitive neuroscientist at the University of Illinois at Urbana-Champaign who studies the phenomenon. "The attitude was, 'Let them sit in their rocking chairs.'"

Instead of reclining in front of the TV, research now shows, adults of all ages who want to maintain sound minds as well as sound bodies should rise from their ruts and exercise both. The more integrated and interesting fitness activities are, the more likely we are to do them, and Kramer's "walking book club" is a cost-effective example: "Discussing the book is intellectually challenging, walking is physical exercise, and social interaction is neuroprotective," he says. "All that's missing is the healthy meal!"

Novelty is crucial to effective cognitive exercise. As Kramer says, "If you've done the *New York Times* crossword for thirty years that might not be such a big help." In contrast, the older adults who came to his lab to learn how to play the cerebral video game Rise of Nations had a new experience for sure. The effort to master the challenge pushed their brains to build fresh neural connections, which made them better gamers. More important, tests showed that the exercise improved their so-called executive control abilities. These vital capacities, such as planning, dealing with ambiguity, and prioritizing, are the very ones that tend to wane earliest in life, yet they're crucial to independent living. "Learning a new language, starting a new hobby, or challenging yourself to do some other thing you haven't done before," says Kramer. "That's the type of activity that's predictive of a good outcome."

The resilience of one group of older professionals whose

life-or-death responsibilities require staying on top of constant change is a strong testimony to the rise-to-the-challenge principle of brain fitness. Despite the stress involved, air-traffic controllers continue to perform well into their sixties. Their demanding work keeps their brains nimble and helps them to stockpile lots of crystallized intelligence. Unlike the fluid sort involved in abilities such as working memory, which start declining at age eighteen, your acquired smarts can improve well into your seventies and help compensate for other cognitive losses. "The controllers in their sixties know all the tricks," says Kramer. "Their wealth of experience and expertise compensates for aging's decrements. And we all have expertise in something!"

You don't have to become a gamer or an air-traffic controller to strengthen your brain with new experiences. You could switch from poker to bridge, bike instead of jog, or do Sudoku instead of the crossword. Going for one of Kramer's twofers, you could invite someone you don't know very well to go for a brisk walk in the park or ask your oldest friend to join you in learning to tap dance. As an added bonus, each time you cultivate your neophilia by trying something different, you make it easier to take the next step away from dull routine. For that matter, just getting up from the recliner and out of the house for a walk or a trip to the gym involves new social and environmental stimuli as well as exercise.

Like mental workouts, the physical sort builds brain as well as muscle mass. Cognitive training affects specific neural networks that make you more receptive to new learning, but the aerobic type, says Kramer, "causes positive brain changes pretty much everywhere you look." A routine that makes you break a sweat actually increases neurogenesis—the growth of new neurons—as well as angiogenesis, or the formation of new blood vessels. Physical effort also raises levels of nerve growth factors and various neurotransmitters, including dopamine, that boost your *élan vital*.

The best news of all is that the impressive mind-body rewards of taking on a new challenge don't require Herculean efforts. Kramer's subjects only commit to walk for an hour three times a week for six months or a year. Despite the fact that they're otherwise free to lie on the couch and gorge on doughnuts, they get substantial benefits in many cognitive functions, which he deems "amazing!" As a result of his findings, if given a magic wand, he'd remodel communities in which you can't walk to shops and other common destinations and strip certain health clubs of their elevators and escalators: "We need more settings that are designed to get us moving, rather than to prevent it."

Pointing to a picture worth a thousand words, which shows a guy "walking" his dog while driving his pickup, Kramer says, "Even now that we have all of this information about how to improve mental fitness, it's a tough sell in America. It's a massive waste of talent not to keep older adults active and productive—not just for them but also for society." Adding a philosophical note, he says, "We can't change our genes, but we can change our lifestyles. We have some control over how well we fare."

. . .

Some provocative, underremarked research conducted by the Russian psychologist Alexander Luria in remote Uzbekistan in 1930 and 1931 offers a vivid illustration of just how profoundly environmental influences affect the expression of neophilia, especially the intellectual and creative sort. He found that the cognitive capacity of illiterate people from small villages was strictly limited to their direct, objective experience of the world. Unlike the educated folk from larger towns, these simple souls were unable to categorize, generalize, or solve problems according to abstract logic. Their mental constraints were such that a villager asked to describe what his neighbor was like wouldn't reply along the subjective lines of "kind" or "unfriendly" but with something like "He plows very straight rows." Needless to say, their stunted experience barred them from the imaginary realms that Alice called "curiouser and curiouser." As one villager put it, "We always speak about things we see. We never speak about the things we did not see."

To understand the environment's role in creativity, it's helpful to compare the development of this human capacity with those of others, such as speech or athleticism. All normal children are born with the neurological ability to speak and write, but those whose parents frequently talk and read to them develop better language skills. Tiger Woods and Venus and Serena Williams started out with strong constitutions and great sensory coordination, but they were also coached from an early age by their ambitious fathers. Cosmonaut Esther

Dyson inherited her renowned physicist father Freeman Dyson's genes, but she also absorbed his intense interest in space and desire to travel there.

The most obvious illustration of experience's effects on original thinking is that no matter how great your innate intelligence, you must work hard and know your stuff before you can do significant creative work. Observing that Watson and Crick discovered DNA's double helix not by generating completely new ideas but by developing existing research, Temple University psychologist Robert Weisberg says, "If you can learn enough about a discipline, you should be able to do original work in it. Creativity is based on thinking *inside* the box." Thus, he says, Lawrence Summers and other inventive minds couldn't fix the recent recession because they have experience with economics but not with an event of the sort that hadn't happened since the Great Depression: "You don't leap out of the box, so if you don't have the right knowledge, you stumble around."

Most creativity researchers disagree with the idea that original thinking requires *only* expertise, but they also emphasize the environment's influence on inventiveness. Mark Runco says that, certain exceptions aside, "if you walked backwards on their developmental paths, you'd find that most creative people were pretty normal kids who might have had something special but also a heck of a lot of opportunity and luck." Offering an analogy, he says, "Your genes predicted that your height would range between five foot ten and six foot two, but it was your diet, health care, and other factors that settled you at six foot one. The same dynamic governs creativity."

Cheryl Rogowski personifies the complex ways in which heredity and experience both early and later in life produce an original thinker. After she earned degrees in business and international studies, instead of taking a job on Wall Street or in Washington, D.C., she stunned her friends by heading back home to take charge of the family onion business in Pine Island, New York. As a farmer's daughter who had acquired financial savvy, she first analyzed local agriculture's status quo and then came up with new ways to improve the environment, the commonweal, and her bottom line.

Instead of sticking to onions, Rogowski decided to grow 250 different vegetables. Many were unusual, and some were especially beloved by low-income ethnic groups hard-pressed to find them in the United States. This expanded variety of crops both increased her base of customers and enriched her soil. In time, she started a catering business that uses local produce, which is healthier for her customers and encourages small farming, and became a leader in the locavore movement. In 2004, Rogowski's flair for finding new ways to do the age-old work of agriculture a stone's throw from Times Square made her the first farmer to win the MacArthur genius award.

The impact of what scientists mildly call "negative life events" offers strong, albeit *noir*ish, testimony to the environment's influence on creativity. When psychologist Dean Simonton reviewed biographical research that chronicled the lives of hundreds of highly inventive people, he found that more than a third had lost a parent before the age of twenty-one, which lends some support to the venerable notion that some are "driven to greatness" by adversity. Isaac Newton is a prime example. He was born prematurely in 1643 after his illiterate father's death and was so small that his mother said he could have fit in a big mug. Then, at the age of three, the fatherless child was separated from her when she remarried, which plunged him into an intense, lifelong state of emotional turmoil that he relieved by immersing himself in work. It's no accident that this driven isolate devised a theory of gravitation that involves action at a distance, so that bodies influence each other without contact. As Simonton says, "His model of the cosmos was like his model of social relationships."

Facing life's vicissitudes early can benefit creative individuals in several ways, starting with encouraging self-reliance. "What other young people have done for them, those who've lost a parent must often do for themselves," says Simonton. "That includes answering questions like 'Who am I? What's important?'" Then, too, a sense of being singled out by fate may make a person less conventional. The advantages of feeling somehow different similarly come across in the fact that being an immigrant or Jewish, as are 30 percent of Nobelists, correlates with original thinking.

The environment not only contributes to shaping your personal expression of neophilia but also helps to determine whether that behavior is an advantage or a disadvantage. A study of a Kenyan tribe called the Ariaals found that the 7R carriers who still live as nomads are better nourished and healthier than those who've moved to towns and settlements. Being hyperactive, distractible, and exploratory apparently gives an edge to someone who must find food and water, ward off raiders, and roll with nature's punches, yet it can be a drawback for one who must sit still and pay attention to schoolwork, farming, or other sedate occupations.

JUST AS YOUR experience can influence your innate temperamental inclinations, culture can shape a population's genetic makeup and thus its mores. Conventional wisdom has it that history is driven by social developments, from new technology like the wheel to new political ideas such as democracy. Proponents of the emerging field of biohistory, however, also see nature's hand in the unfolding human narrative. One of their most interesting arguments focuses on the neophiliac 7R allele's radically uneven global distribution.

Research conducted at the University of California at Irvine by Robert Moyzis and his collaborators offers a provocative explanation for why some populations around the world have very high incidence of 7R and others, a very low one. A study led by psychologist Chuansheng Chen first posited that the allele began as a "migration gene." Restlessness can be a big benefit in certain situations, and Moyzis, who takes the sudden-and-recent view of behavioral evolution, thinks that the mutation helped *Homo sapiens* survive and thrive by spurring our vast African exodus to distant parts unknown.

Everyone who carries the 7R gene today, whether a European urbanite, a sub-Saharan villager, or a South American Indian, has essentially the same version, and using standard statistical methods for analyzing DNA sequences, Moyzis determined that 7R probably arose about 50,000 to 40,000 years ago, right around the time of the great migrations. Pointing out that the allele is relatively new and that other primates don't have it at all, he says, "To have maintained a significant incidence in the current population, it must have been selected for, because if a mutation has no benefit, evolution will get rid of it."

Studies of populations around the world show that the groups whose forebears stayed closest to our African home at the time of the great migrations have a high incidence of our ancestral DRD4-4 allele, whose strong affinity for dopamine translates into strong regulation of behavioral excitability. In contrast, the descendants of those who traveled the farthest have the greatest frequency of the genetic variants linked to a low affinity for dopamine and robust novelty seeking: 2R, 5R, and especially 7R. As much as 25 percent of the population in much of Europe, as well as their American descendants, carry 7R, but its highest incidence—up to 85 percent in some groups—occurs among the South American Indian tribes who live farthest from Africa in areas such as the Amazon basin.

At first, it's hard to believe the research that shows that the novelty-seeking 7R allele hardly exists in China anymore. Moyzis thinks that it mutated into the much shorter 2R version, which suggests a selection *against* the most neophiliac variant. The educated guess as to why and how such a genetic shift occurred in China is "cultural selection" by whatever means. (Offering a seemingly tongue-in-cheek example, University of Utah anthropologist and biohistorian Henry Harpending recalls that when he asked a Chinese biogeneticist why the allele had almost disappeared, "without hesitating, the researcher said, 'Oh, we killed all the 7R people.'") In one scenario, the Asian adventurers who carried the restless allele might have crossed the Bering Strait into the Americas, where its incidence is high. In another proposed by the Moyzis group, as China's society settled into an economy in which many people spent most of the day cultivating rice, a restless mind and an appetite for novelty became drawbacks. Even two thousand years ago, China's mandarin system would have favored the individuals likeliest to get ahead in its bureaucracy, so that unlike his friskier brother, a dutiful son who rose up in the ranks might have acquired multiple wives and produced many offspring.

Whatever its roots in the ancient past, China's traditionally conservative society is very different from, say, America's freewheeling, risk-tolerant, inventive culture. In November 2010, the Chinese government, keenly aware of the country's reputation for imitation rather than innovation, announced a program for dramatically increasing its low number of patents. By offering incentives such as cash bonuses and better housing, the leadership hopes to produce more creators of technology like the iPad rather than just efficient manufacturers of them.

It may sound politically incorrect, but over the past few thousand years, cultures and their differences appear to have influenced human DNA, especially in Asia. As Harpending puts it, "When I first saw that research relating an interesting and normal behavioral phenotype to a gene difference, I thought to myself, 'Pandora's box is open now.'" This phenomenon is all the more fascinating when you consider that although the two populations are now so diametrically different in both 7R's frequency and the agendas of their societies, the New World Indians are thought to be the descendants of Asians who migrated there perhaps 12,000 years ago. The same hyper, distractible, risk-taking characteristics associated with the allele that poorly suit traditional Chinese culture can be highly adaptive in other settings, from the Amazon basin to Silicon Valley, where selection could work in 7R's favor.

The history of 7R in China prompts speculation about its future in the increasingly sedentary, screen-oriented, postindustrial West. In our desk-tethered world, it's already hard to believe that it wasn't so long ago in human history that most people, much less small children, weren't expected to spend their days sitting still and concentrating on mental tasks for hours on end. Unlike Amazon tribesmen and rural Ariaals, many young novelty seekers in our urbanized environments lack the legitimate outlets for their high spirits long provided by our species' ancient, traditional pursuits of exploration and hunting. If also poorly raised and immature, they can end up making trouble for themselves and others. As Harpending says, "There are badly behaved kids who will pick up a brick and throw it through a store window, even though they're sure to get caught. It's just a way of relieving their own boredom."

Now that college has become a middle-class mandate, although no longer a guarantee of a good job, it's easy to forget that many bright, energetic novelty seekers who couldn't afford or didn't relish higher education once enjoyed well-paid, productive careers working in factories and on farms. Many of those jobs have moved overseas or become highly mechanized, but in the relatively recent past, such workers came up with countless innovations that helped to fuel America's industrial dominance. Recalling an uncle who was a tool-and-die maker and often earned more from ideas that he put in the plant's suggestion box than he did from wages, Harpending says, "There are differences out there, and we ought not to force everyone to learn calculus. Our rewards system, which is based on cognitive elitism, is all screwed up. Maybe a good surgeon should make twice as much as a cabinet-maker or other skilled worker, but not twenty times as much."

IF CULTURE CAN affect a population's neophilia through heredity, as it has in China, it much more often does so by influencing manners and mores. Imagine your life as a Muslim sometime during Islam's Golden Age, which lasted from the ninth to the twelfth century C.E. You'd belong to an energetic, outward-looking, cosmopolitan young culture that was the world's creative dynamo. Perhaps you'd study with one of its fabled *hakims*, or polymathic Renaissance men. Maybe its brilliant science, philosophy, art, medicine, or industry would inspire you to produce an important contribution of your own.

If you were a Muslim of the thirteenth century, however, you'd live in a very different world. A still-mysterious convergence of negative environmental forces, including the Mongol and Turkic invasions, plague, and a new, revelation-oriented religious conservatism, was already undermining Islam's vi-brant, progressive society. The culture increasingly withdrew into itself, gave up on progress, and shut out the rest of the world for centuries. No matter what your innate inclinations and gifts, the chances that you'd be able to express your neo-philia by learning exciting new things and doing innovative work would have tragically diminished.

*Seven*

# Culture, Curiosity, and Boredom

NEOPHILIA ENABLED EARLY *Homo sapiens* to adapt to droughts and floods, experiment with new technology, and venture into unknown territory in search of resources. By 10,000 years ago, however, many of our ancestors had left behind the wild, free life of the hunter-gatherers to become farmers dwelling in settlements. Living in large groups increased intellectual stimulation as well as safety, and our early agrarian forebears could devote more of their explorative energy to creative achievements both cerebral and practical. Around 8,000 years ago, they invented written symbols to represent words, for example, and 3,000 years later, sanitary drains and public baths. On the other hand, big populations also required more rules and regulations for keeping order, which gave rise to what we've come to think of as "the establishment." Then as now, the powers that be surely imposed limits on novelty seeking and cast unauthorized questions and quests as crude, subversive, or even heretical.

The surprising history of curiosity testifies to society's strong influence in determining whether neophilia is a virtue or vice. Even the philosophical Greeks and Romans were wary of inquiring too deeply into the way things are. Christianity only intensified this ancient fear that such hubris would provoke the gods and disturb the status quo. To the church, an inquiring mind signified a preference for the worldly over the spiritual and for human knowledge over divine revelation. The consequences of Pandora's desire to know what was inside that eponymous box and Eve's curiosity about the aptly named forbidden fruit of the Tree of Knowledge showed that a keen interest in new things, ideas, and experiences could upset the higher authorities. "The desire to search for something hidden by God for good reason was a deliberate violation of the order of things," says Barbara Benedict, who has studied curiosity's literary history. In an era of rigidly stratified classes, asking too many questions was regarded as insubordinate in the social as well as religious sphere. "To uncover what is hidden was associated with ambition," she says. "By wanting to know more and be more than other people, you were overstepping your status."

Like individual rights, the concept of curiosity as a laudable urge to learn new things and to know and understand for yourself is a modern innovation of the Age of Reason. In the early eighteenth century, the philosopher John Locke's revolutionary new way of looking at the world generated a tidal wave of intellectual neophilia. His theory of empiricism stated that true knowledge is based not on faith or revelation but on experience, ideally supported by evidence or experimentation. This bold assertion was a giant step toward establishing science's primacy in determining truth and our modern ideas about the self's uniqueness and importance. "You were no longer subject to inherited ideas implanted in you by God but learned through your own senses and reflection," says Benedict. "Almost like a little god, you had the ability to make your own identity by experiencing the world around you."

The accelerating Industrial Revolution complemented Enlightenment philosophy in encouraging neophilia, starting with swelling the ranks of a prosperous, independent-minded middle class. Europe's booming imperialistic economies expanded its citizens' worldview by flooding the market with exotic commodities from foreign parts as well as mass-produced goods, including the first cheap books, which circulated the latest incendiary ideas and adventurous stories. It's no accident that Daniel Defoe's *Robinson Crusoe* (1719), which chronicled the protagonist's New World encounters with the novel and different, became a best seller. Upset by these challenges to the established order, the aristocracy stepped up its snobbism, one expression of which was the invention of the literary canon.

Reactionaries notwithstanding, the West's new mode of open-minded thinking transformed the old social system. Even some wealthy grandees abandoned their traditional class roles to take up shockingly novel pursuits, such as assembling the first scientific collections. Gathering and treasuring rocks, fossils, and other things previously thought worthless was "an incredibly arrogant thing to do," says Benedict. "The collectors were saying, 'We find beauty and meaning in new things that previous generations have found to be valueless and hideous.'"

Enlightenment neophilia and its show-me approach to life had an even more galvanizing effect on society's lower and middle strata. Increased literacy helped to advance the idea that anyone of any station could choose what to buy, read, and think—even women. Curious females had long been regarded as insubordinates who, like Eve and Pandora, sought status through control over men. Suddenly, however, an inquisitive mind was no longer a sign of overstepping your place, says Benedict, "but a demonstration that you could create your *own* place. A whole new class of people, including women, who weren't conventionally educated yet wanted to understand the world was enfranchised."

The burgeoning, upwardly mobile bourgeoisie could increasingly afford to shift its focus from brute survival to the enjoyment of a more elaborate emotional and intellectual life, as evidenced by the invention of the novel (from the Italian *novella,* or piece of news) and other popular entertainments. As the Romantic movement's stirrings further exalted subjective feelings, people grew even more interested in their own and others' consciousness, and the English language began to reflect these major social and psychological changes.

*Curiosity* had previously referred to a rare, foreign, or

artfully made object that might be kept in a "curiosity cabinet." In the new cultural climate, however, the term was also applied to an inquiring state of mind, and even to the person who cultivated it. Samuel Butler came up with a much-repeated jest about one of the new scientific collectors: "His dotage upon curiosities at length renders him one of them." *Interesting* underwent a similar evolution. The word had traditionally meant "important" and was also applied to objects, such as an artwork. By the turn of the nineteenth century, however, the Enlightenment's emphasis on individuality and Romanticism's stress on personal expressiveness had transformed the term, which now referred to one's subjective evaluation of something's capacity to draw and hold one's attention—an increasingly important concern.

It's easy to be patronizing about the past's quaint attitudes, but the way in which we regard neophilic curiosity still often depends on the circumstances. Americans applaud inquisitiveness in the schoolroom and the sciences but not where our money and sex lives are concerned. In many modern cultures, questioning is considered rude, even a character flaw. In buttoned-up England, says Benedict, "it's even bad manners to ask someone what he does."

WHETHER VILIFIED OR PRAISED, curiosity about the new and unfamiliar has long been with us. However, the very different state of boredom—the unpleasant sense of there being nothing that interests you—is largely a modern condition that still doesn't exist in much of the world. Situations that would strike us as unbearably dull, say, waiting for hours or even days for a bus, are considered just the way life is in many developing nations. Anthropologist Henry Harpending has done extensive fieldwork in the backcountries of Namibia and Botswana, where in most ways, he says, "folks are just like you and me. But one thing that the Westerners who go there just can't understand and are open-mouthed about is the people's tolerance for tedium. They can just sit all day under the trees. This ability to do nothing is just alien to us." He's fluent in Bushman and has tried for twenty years to elicit a word for boredom, but the closest he has gotten is an unsatisfactory *tired*.

Although neophiliacs are especially subject to boredom, our increasingly fidgety behavior in queues and other public settings suggests that the whole culture's threshold for tedium lowers by the day. Forced to withstand more than a few minutes in one of the shrinking number of places not wired for perpetual TV, we fiddle with our smart gadgets, hoping for a headline, text, or ball-game score to check, and only resort to the old-fashioned pastime of daydreaming as a last recourse. Creativity researcher Oshin Vartanian describes an all-too-believable scene in a car dealer's waiting room in which clients were forced to endure television deprivation for up to thirty minutes. "We just can't do that anymore!" he says. "Everyone was going crazy, trying to turn on a broken TV."

Our voracious appetite for new stimuli makes it hard for us to believe that the seeming invulnerability to boredom displayed by the Bushmen and others in nonindustrial societies was once the rule and still persists in certain subcultures in the West. In winter, many farmers in the northern latitudes engage in a kind of quasi-hibernation not unlike that of Alaska's Inuit, which involves mostly staying inside not doing much of anything. "It looks to outsiders like depression," says Harpending, "but it's just getting your activity level down. This behavior isn't rooted in the genes, because I'm not five generations removed from people who could sit on the porch and not move for four hours. In fact, my grandmother wasn't bad at it, and the difference between me and my grandmother is cultural."

Like the history of curiosity, the chronology of boredom testifies to neophilia's modern expansion. A friend's offhand remark that her French mother had described boredom as "a sin" sent Patricia Meyer Spacks, then a professor of literature at Yale, to the *Oxford English Dictionary*. There she discovered two interesting things. *Boredom* has no derivation: That is, it doesn't come from any other word but was specially created. Moreover, the term didn't appear in English until the later eighteenth century, long after the French spoke of *ennui*. Curious about why England would have suddenly needed such a word, Spacks set about examining *boredom* in literature from the eighteenth century onward. The historian and man of letters Horace Walpole was the first to write the term, which may have been a slangy upper-class pun on the bore as a figurative boar. *Boredom* soon cropped up in other texts, suggesting that it had caught on in everyday speech.

Like the transformation of curiosity from virtue to vice

to virtue again, the ascendance of the psychological state of boredom reflects vast cultural changes. As people became more interested in their inner lives, they required a new vocabulary that emphasized the individual's internal responses to the world, rather than its external stimuli. "When you invent a word for something," says Spacks, "in a sense you're inventing the thing itself, even though the experience came first. Once the word existed, I think the experience of boredom—the incapacity to get pleasure or meaning from your experience—became very much more widespread."

At first, boredom was considered to be a moral and intellectual failure on the part of individuals who couldn't keep themselves engaged or entertained. By declaring that "when a man is tired of London, he is tired of life," Samuel Johnson (1709–84) asserted that it's your own fault if you can't find things to interest you. Spacks's study of letters by upper-class women of his day shows that despite the severe social constraints imposed on them, they agreed with the good doctor.

If any group in history needed a term to describe stultifying experience, it would seem to have been well-off eighteenth-century Englishwomen. Their activities and aspirations were unimaginably circumscribed. By way of illustration, Spacks says that the male author of one of the era's many guides to conduct and manners advises his daughters to learn sewing and embroidery, "but not to think that it would have any value or usefulness! It would just be something for them to do to fill up their empty time." However, the letters of the era's wealthy wives and widows of a certain age show that despite the strictures imposed upon them, they took responsibility for the quality of their lives, arranged to spend a lot of time enjoying one another's company, and weren't in the least bored. Indeed, Spacks says, "moralists of the day worried that these women were having an awful lot of fun." Young unmarried ladies, who had less freedom than the merry widows and their peers, contrived at least one strategy to avoid ennui. "The moralists were very concerned that they were reading novels, which could give them 'ideas,'" she says. "That suggests that these women might have otherwise experienced their lives as empty."

In a highly consequential yet underremarked shift that's the foundation of our own media-driven culture, the Enlightenment conviction that boredom was an internal problem and your own damned fault began to weaken. Tedium was increasingly blamed on social and physical environments that failed to engage you. In one literary example of this trend, Charles Dickens first referred to boredom in a pamphlet written in 1836, in which he attributed workingmen's drunkenness on Sundays to the Sabbath's lack of structure; by 1852, however, he used the term six times in *Bleak House*. In 1892, the horrors of boredom were so well established that in "The Yellow Wallpaper," the American writer Charlotte Perkins Gilman blamed a woman's descent into madness on her physician husband's decision to keep her locked in her bedroom because of a "slight hysterical tendency."

Boredom came into its own as a major literary subject in the twentieth century. The existentialist philosophers regarded it as *the* human condition, reflecting a void at life's core. Here is Martin Heidegger: "Profound boredom, drifting here and there in the abysses of our existence like a muffling fog, removes all things and men and oneself along with it into a remarkable indifference. This boredom reveals being as a whole." Anticipating the 1980s rock song "Love Is a Stranger in an Open Car," the influential psychologist Erich Fromm declared that sex and automobiles were important vehicles for the relief of postmodern tedium.

In the twenty-first century, few would agree with Oscar Wilde's old-fashioned assertion that ennui is "the one sin for which there is no forgiveness." As Spacks says, "The need to be stimulated at every moment by something outside ourselves is characteristic of our time and place. The proliferation of electronics is largely about providing entertainment and communications every minute." Despite the popular conviction that entitlement to engaging stimuli is part of the Bill of Rights or ought to be, she upholds Dr. Johnson's view: "I was taught that 'interesting' doesn't say anything about an object, but rather, something about a person's feeling. Boredom has to do with a subjective experience rather than objective fact."

Not so long ago, parents and teachers used to admonish children with maxims such as "The idle mind is the devil's workshop." Spacks recalls feeling "a real sense of rage if my daughter complained about having nothing to do, and she became an extremely creative artist who doesn't know the meaning of boredom." At a recent dinner, Spacks was stunned when a young colleague situated her six-month-old infant in the middle of the table, so that the child would be stimulated. "If I hadn't seen it, I wouldn't have believed it possible," she says. "You learn very early either that you have to make life interesting for yourself or that someone else has to make it interesting for you. Which way you see that issue makes an enormous difference."

ATTITUDES ABOUT NOVELTY and change not only shift over time but also vary from culture to culture. Some simply react to new things when they must, even if only to suppress them, while others actively seek and strive to produce them. In sixteenth-century Florence, for example, a creative explosion was ignited by its extraordinary artistic talent, which was supported by a progressive civic society that was open to many forms of novelty, from the booming Oriental trade to the new humanistic philosophy. In twenty-first-century Japan, which historically hasn't often welcomed outsiders or innovative influences into its homogeneous, insular society, the most popular cultural activity is karaoke.

# Eight

# The Ever-New Frontier

FOR BETTER AND WORSE, the United States is history's most neophilic culture. Indeed, Mark Twain complained that the word *new* was so routinely used in connection with America "that we early and permanently retain the impression that there is nothing old about it." Summing up the national modus operandi, the artist Maira Kalman writes: "Don't mope in your room. Go invent something. That is the American message. Electricity. Flight. The telephone. Television. Computers. It never stops."

The experience of its first peoples provides a thought-provoking context and contrast for that American credo. Much like our evolutionary African ancestors, these tribes primarily used neophilia for its original purpose of adapting to environmental change. When he's not seated behind Margaret Mead's old desk at New York City's American Museum of Natural History, anthropologist David Hurst Thomas is roaming the high country of California, Nevada, and Wyoming, trying to understand the lives of mysterious Native American tribes sometimes called the "mountain Shoshoni." Despite the unpredictable weather extremes, air thin enough to cause altitude sickness, and limited natural resources, they chose to build part-time settlements above twelve thousand feet in the remotest reaches of the high alpine desert. That this draconian step makes no sense, at least at first, poses the question behind Thomas's research. "What are they reacting to?" he says. "Why are they doing something that seems so irrational?"

One of these "high-rise villages," nestled in the upper reaches of Wyoming's Wind River Mountains, was settled as far back as 1,500 years ago, and possibly much earlier, by a people known only as the "sheep eaters." Their familial groups of perhaps twenty to thirty members built sturdy if makeshift wooden shelters equipped with fire pits, and made simple artifacts, including weapons, pottery, and now-enigmatic petroglyphs, or images engraved in rock. Along with roots and pine nuts, their major food source was the high peaks' abundant bighorn sheep.

Any intrepid modern hiker panting his or her way up the mountain to the site of the sheep eaters' village would soon agree that the logical place for them to have lived would have been the sheltered river valley some six thousand feet below. Down there, the weather is milder, the breathing easier, and fish and other game plentiful. When they had a yen for some mutton, the tribe could have sent a few hunters into the mountains for a tasty bighorn or two. Instead of following this sensible plan, however, whole families, from children to grandparents, chose to spend all but the coldest months pursuing a labor-intensive way of life in a harsh habitat.

Evidence increasingly suggests that the sheep eaters' seemingly counterintuitive lifestyle was a sophisticated adaptation to environmental change. Between A.D. 400 or 500 and about A.D. 1300, a dramatic global event known as the medieval climatic anomaly wracked large parts of the Northern Hemisphere with what Thomas describes as "off-the-chart" climate shifts, particularly extreme drought, the likes of which had been rare there before and haven't been seen since. In the American West's high country, water would have been scarce everywhere, and the competition for it among the region's tribes would have been fierce. Archeological evidence suggests that this era was indeed a violent time, during which the sheep eaters would have had to contend with their more bellicose rivals, such as the ancestral Crow tribe. Thus, they were forced to confront *Homo sapiens'* two classic options for coping with environmental change. As Thomas says, "You just cut out and go someplace else, or you make do by coming up with new solutions for survival."

The sheep eaters adopted an interesting blend of both approaches. Horizontal migration was pointless in a region full of hostile competitors, so they moved vertically instead. This decision in turn led them to create a new high-altitude lifestyle suited to their secure, defensible mountain fortress.

Their efforts were aided by a powerful new technology that became what Thomas calls a "game changer" throughout much of the world.

The invention of the bow and arrow might be the exception that proves one of anthropology's recently formulated rules. "We used to think that it took some lone genius living in the fertile crescent to create something important, like agriculture," says Thomas. "Now we understand that such major things were invented dozens and dozens of times around the world." However, the bow and arrow, which he calls "one of the greatest innovations since the Ice Age," is such a complex tool that he and many of his colleagues believe that it could only have been designed once. Then, as different groups saw the new weapon, they adapted it to their local culture and conditions.

The bow and arrow appears to have entered the Northern Hemisphere via the Bering Strait at some point later than 2,000 years ago, which corresponds with rough estimates of the high-rise villages' beginnings. Without it, the sheep eaters' way of life would have been far more difficult, if not impossible. Previously, the men would have hunted in groups of six or so, trying to get close enough to throw a dart-pointed spear at a fleet-footed bighorn able to bound up steep cliffs. If this grueling group effort succeeded, the hunters would have shared the meat among their families.

Armed with a bow made from the strong, curved horns of their favorite prey, however, one sheep eater could shoot and kill a big animal from a distance. This vastly more efficient way of hunting changed the tribe's culture, first and foremost by enabling them to secure adequate food without descending to the dangerous valley below. However, the innovative tool would also have inspired lots of new ideas, starting with different rules for the ownership and storage of meat. As Thomas says, "The bow and arrow didn't just bring a different way to hunt. It may have spawned an entirely new lifestyle."

Long after the high-rise villages were established, all the Native American peoples were forced to respond to a major environmental change, this time imposed by culture rather than nature. Before the arrival of the Europeans, most tribes sensibly preferred to live near the coasts and along major rivers, where food, fuel, and other necessities were plentiful. By the eighteenth and nineteenth centuries, however, the white newcomers provided serious competition for these resources. Once again, groups confronting challenges to their traditional ways of life faced two stark choices: move or stay put and try to adapt to the new situation.

The tribes who would become known as the Plains Indians first chose the "move" option. It's a big country, and some groups, including the Cheyenne, Comanche, Crow, and Sioux, headed to the Great Basin area, which is bounded by the Mississippi River and the Rockies, Canada and Texas. Just as the sheep eaters' new high-rise lifestyle was enabled by the bow and arrow, the Plains tribes' adaptation to their new environment was enhanced by a new four-legged tool brought to the Americas by the early Spanish explorers. By the eighteenth century, these Indians had captured wild horses descended from the conquistadors' mounts, become skilled equestrians—especially the Comanche—and created a new and stunningly short-lived way of life that still captivates imaginations around the world.

Hunters on foot are limited to relatively small territories and game, but mounted they can range far and kill big animals like the buffalo. Accordingly, the Plains groups developed semi-nomadic and nomadic equestrian cultures oriented around the bison, which now provided much of their food, clothing, and even shelter in the form of the portable hide tepee. Like the bow and arrow before it, the horse ushered in much more than just a new way to hunt. Easier travel enabled mounted warriors to invade one another's territories and fight more effectively, but it also allowed for more interactions among different groups, which increased their exposure to new ideas and ways of doing things.

By the 1850s, the Plains Indians' innovative, fabled way of life was already endangered by the incursions of railroads, settlers, prospectors, and the buffalo hunters who almost wiped out the animal on which their entire culture was based. By 1890, the sixty million bison that had roamed in 1800 had been reduced to 750. Such catastrophic change left many tribes, including the Wind River sheep eaters' impoverished descendants, once again facing the classic choices. They moved, or were driven, onto reservations, where they began the long struggle to adapt to an alien culture based on private property instead of communal resources and agriculture rather than hunting.

. . .

INSPIRED BY THE eighteenth century's wave of neophilia, the Europeans who were adventurous enough to migrate to America and their descendants set about developing a new political way of life, and defended it with a revolution. Notwithstanding their radical ideas, however, life in their agrarian society moved slowly outside of its few big cities, and occasions for excitement were few and far between.

Then, in the mid nineteenth century, the technological and social developments of the accelerating Industrial Revolution began to inject hefty doses of novelty and change into American life. Public entertainment is an interesting example. Previously, people who lived on farms and in small towns and villages had had little to enliven their monotonous routines beyond the occasional big-tent revival meeting. With the advent of the railroad, however, even remote areas without decent roads could enjoy P. T. Barnum's "traveling circus." Its mind-boggling novelties ranged from General Tom Thumb to Jumbo the elephant, from the Fee-gee mermaid to the soprano Jenny Lind, aka the "Swedish Nightingale." Easier, faster travel also meant that the high-minded upper middle class could indulge its more refined tastes by attending the Chautauqua circuit's seasonal assemblies and group discussions of the latest intellectual and political ideas.

By the early twentieth century, the amount of novelty in American life had increased almost unimaginably. Moreover, Thomas Edison's electric light, Henry Ford's inexpensive Model T car (known as the "flivver"), and Alexander Graham Bell's telephone not only were revolutionary inventions in themselves but also greatly expanded the potential for all kinds of new experiences. From the 1920s onward, a surge of mass production enabled by plastics and other innovative technologies suddenly yielded many, many more new things to buy (and lots of today's collectibles). The growth of Hollywood and radio broadcasting, followed by television in the forties, elicited a chorus of neophobic protests about the impossibility of keeping up that has grown louder with each passing decade.

No less than those of previous generations, our expressions of neophilia are profoundly influenced by our cultural milieu, perhaps much more than we like to imagine. One obvious example is our twenty-first-century hunger for new stuff, which would astonish our great-grandparents, if not our grandparents. This voracious appetite is fed by ferocious global economic competition, now waged by China, India, Brazil, and other rapidly developing countries as well as Western nations, that forces companies to, as the Silicon Valley mantra puts it, "innovate or die." As a result, we confront a seemingly unlimited selection of new goods that become old almost as soon as they're out of the box, and there's no end in sight to this proliferation. By the lights of the old Protestant ethic, *consumer* meant something like "spendthrift" or "squanderer." The avid customers queuing up for Black Friday sales and the latest Apple products, however, resemble religious pilgrims who prove their devotion by sleeping in front of the shrine on the night before they're permitted to purchase the Holy Grail.

One bright side of our pursuit of the latest, coolest stuff is that many of those products are information machines that, if used wisely, can help us use our neophilia to learn and create worthwhile new things. Our passion for these clever tools has given Robert Kozinets, an anthropologist who studies consumer culture, marketing, and media at Canada's York University, an intriguing question to study: "Why are we drawn to buy the slightly smaller MP3 player or the laptop in a different color with the slightly bigger screen, when the stuff we have still works and mostly all that's really different is its newness?"

Until very recently, geeks weren't cool, and neither was technology. One major reason for the ascendance of both is that our new information gadgets are imbued with a quality that Kozinets calls "techspressiveness." Since the Industrial Revolution, we've mostly regarded technological advances favorably, as both boons to efficiency and beacons of social progress (notwithstanding the nineteenth-century Luddites and their sympathizers in the modern green and off-the-grid movements, who regard them as a threat to nature and tradition). However, it took a new, sexy breed of electronics to turn tech into a cultural obsession.

From the mid-1980s onward, smaller yet ever more powerful and versatile phones, laptops, and the like began to transcend mere toolness to become something closer to a gearhead's Corvette Sting Ray or a fashionista's Birkin bag. No longer simply useful, techspressive machines are now also important identity and status signifiers, which assemble your selection of brands, apps, playlists, and photos into a kind of self-portrait. As Kozinets says, "It's not just this technology's innate newness that makes it so interesting but also the channeling of that novelty into new areas, such as personal expression."

Our bottomless cornucopia of new stuff brings many rewards. Who wants to go back to pay phones and giant black-and-white TVs with tiny, snowy screens? However, this horn of plenty also exacts a cost beyond the products' price tags, starting with the marketplace's increasing dominance of our culture and behavior. "Everything moves through the market now in a way that didn't happen even a generation ago," says Kozinets. He offers a homely illustration: His teenage son doesn't want generic shampoo in his bathroom, lest a friend notice that it's not the "right" brand. Evoking thoughts of the so-called eBay, Apple, and craigslist nations, he says, "We increasingly direct society through our consumerism, using dollars as votes. *On the material level, that's how we manifest as a species now*" [author's italics].

The most obvious way in which the market influences your behavior is to get you to buy things whether you need them or not. There's nothing new about this effort per se. All of the ads you're exposed to each day—five thousand now, up from one thousand in 1970—try to trigger a dopaminergic surge of *wanting* in your brain, and so did Benjamin Franklin back in 1742, when he printed America's first magazine ads. It has been more than a century since that great hustler Barnum said, "There's a sucker born every minute."

What *is* different is marketing's and advertising's increasing sophistication and subtlety in appealing to your emotions, aspirations, and sense of who you are to get into your purse. This advance in these darkish arts, which began with the original *Mad Men*'s so-called creative revolution of the 1960s, was exemplified by classic campaigns such as McDonald's "You deserve a break today" and Nike's "Just do it." This new type of pitch almost skipped flacking the product to appeal to deep human yearnings and invest the brand with a meaning far beyond mere utility. In the witty documentary *Art & Copy,* one ace adman explains what consumers *really* hope to get from that Coach handbag or Hermès tie: "What they're buying is what they wish their lives would be."

The strategy of "experience engineering" turns the venerable art of influencing your behavior by blurring the lines between the way life is and the way you'd like it to be into something like a science. Indeed, its experts can even employ neuromarketing, or the use of neurological and other biometric measurements to gauge consumers' engagement with a product. The ad firms and marketers who practice it develop and promote products not just for their efficiency, say, or solid value, but also as sources of personal transformation and vehicles of transcendence. Thus, your Starbucks latte or Whole Foods salad isn't just an overpriced caffeinated beverage or low-cal lunch but also a special product that offers a special moment to a special person: a Starbucks or Whole Foods kind of person.

To be fair, the market's hip, experience-oriented pitches aren't forced on hapless consumers by evil geniuses bent on mind control. "We want these special new products and experiences," says Kozinets, "and marketers and companies respond to that want. We've made this system together, and now it's making us." Observing that if people stopped buying the latest sine qua non gadgets, companies wouldn't keep churning them out, he particularly disputes the notion that sophisticated twenty-first-century consumers are being duped into buying the latest thing: "In our culture now, the idea that novelty distinguishes people as innovative, risk-taking, and cool has attained a life of its own."

The tacit cooperation between experience engineers and neophilic consumers has also transformed the marketplace from vehicle of crass commerce to agent of personal growth. As Kozinets says, "The market now has this element of sacredness. Companies try to build on that feeling, so that consumers will form a religion-like affiliation around their product." The stunning phenomenon of American Girl dolls—elaborate, expensive toys that become even more so as their many accessories are acquired—offers insight into how experience engineering can pull at your heartstrings and open your wallet. What the manufacturer is *really* selling isn't so much a doll, says Kozinets, "as a family experience and a sacred moment of bonding. If you travel to one of their special stores to create a special memory with your daughter, you don't think twice about dropping $230, which is the average sale." Like the consumers who make the pilgrimage to purchase the emotion-enriched dolls, the women who sign up on waiting lists for the privilege of overpaying for the latest Tod's bag or Prada shoe buy into the notion that the more effort it takes to get the product and its religious experience, the more special both will be.

If Apple is the iconic brand squared, Steve Jobs was the Leonardo of experience engineering. "In an eerie way," says anthropologist Grant McCracken, "that company reaches into our expectations and crafts machines that seem to know what features we want just as they occur to us. That's the result of very careful ethnographic user interface research and smart design that's tested and tested. Steve says, 'No, that still won't do, it's not easy or smart or sexy enough.' Then his people do it over again." If only by default, Apple's competitors must also be skillful experience engineers. Microsoft's PC-versus-Mac advertisements, which play with the cultural stereotypes of who's cool and who's not, are a good example. "With something like genius," says McCracken, "Microsoft shows supposedly not-hip people, like a little Korean girl, using Microsoft products to engage in their own creativity and just not caring about their hipness. That positions Apple as being a little too precious."

Some of the cleverest examples of experience engineering involve making new products seem old, sort of. "What moves those of genius, what inspires their work is not new ideas," said Eugène Delacroix, "but their obsession with the idea that what has already been said is still not enough." The artist might have been describing the way in which venerable brands such as Harley-Davidson, Levi Strauss, and BMW stay competitive by draping their latest wares in a symbolic retro mantle that evokes the good old days. Kozinets points to the Volkswagen Beetle's recent reincarnation as a prime example of "re-envisioning the physical product but keeping some of the symbolic continuity." The car's exterior was carefully tweaked to retain its flower-power vibe even though its mechanical components were completely redesigned. To underscore that the new bug was not just some car, its promotional slogan was "The people want a true icon."

If Delacroix is right in saying that skillfully blending the old and the new is a kind of innovative genius in itself, then the couturier Karl Lagerfeld is a veritable Picasso. Over the past decades, he has invented countless instantly recognizable yet of-the-moment iterations of Coco Chanel's braid-trimmed suit, quilted purse, and other classics. As Kozinets says, "Creativity works well within constraints, and people can distinguish it better. The unlimited sort often doesn't pan out so well."

Even some enterprises that at first glance seem to have only pure, altruistic motivations use experience engineering to lure high-minded us into purchasing new stuff. Burning Man began as a free, countercultural festival held in Nevada's Black Rock desert, but tickets now cost hundreds of dollars. The event's Web site appears at first to shun vulgar commerce, yet it includes a "marketplace" that hustles T-shirts, calendars, and the like, as well as links to businesses that sell the maps, guides, and equipment you need in order to spend a week in the wilds. To Kozinets, Burning Man offers a lesson in "how to use the Net to create the expectations and the meaning that consumers can realize when they commit to the product."

If buying yet another pair of sneakers because you've been engineered into thinking they'll make you cool is one problem, trying to figure out exactly which style to choose is another. As Swarthmore psychologist Barry Schwartz has written, the continual decision making involved in sorting through the market's overflowing basket squanders our finite stores of time and attention on what are mostly trivial distinctions and distractions. Now that various media advise us what to buy—and others tell us how to cull our jammed closets, drawers, and garages—deciding on a sound system or computer can turn into a massive research project, if not a paralyzing approach-avoidance conflict. Even minor purchases can be exhausting when what were once simple choices—black loafers or brown, Levis or Wranglers—become brain drains. The supermarket's selection of cereals alone has expanded from a couple of shelves of corn flakes, Wheaties, and Cheerios to an aisle seemingly the length of a football field. Even if you know that you want Cheerios, you have to decide which kind: Regular, Honey Nut, MultiGrain, Banana Nut, Crunch, Berry Burst, Frosted, Apple Cinnamon, Fruity, or Yogurt Burst. If you stick with trusty Honey Nut, will you be missing out on a better experience offered by a newer product?

These daily decision-making dramas imposed by too much pointless novelty repeatedly put us at the mercy of what behavioral economists call the focusing illusion: Simply by thinking about something, you will exaggerate its importance. In other words, when you confront a selection of microwaves or down jackets, you will overemphasize their differences, not because they necessarily matter but simply because they exist and you're considering them. The longer you brood, the more even small distinctions—the stainless-steel finish or the black enamel? the Velcro tabs or the zippers?—will fog over the items' probable essential sameness, sap your finite mental resources, and set you up for buyer's regret. More important, after the first five minutes of ownership, the outcome of all that effort is likely to make little or no difference in the quality of your daily experience.

THE LARGER PROBLEM that underlies the pursuit of new things just because they're new isn't the waste of time and money but the fact that we've lost touch with neophilia's purpose. This great gift isn't meant to push us to buy stuff we don't need or to seek constant entertainment but to help us adapt to change, from the economy's volatility to the climate crisis, and to learn about and create useful new things. For you, that could mean anything from upgrading your career skills to buying a hybrid car or designing a solar-heating scheme for your home. For society, the right-minded exercise of neophilia would require getting serious about fixing the entitlement programs, creating jobs, and securing energy independence, but novelty of this vital sort is in short supply.

There are various reasons for our current neophilia crisis, which boils down to "too much dumb new stuff, not enough good new ideas." Many of us are too distracted by the floods of trivial yet instantly gratifying novelty to focus on the serious sort; that's why a recent president could tell us to contribute to the nation's war effort by heading to the mall. Then too, America is still reeling from a long, scary economic slump that put an end to two decades of expansion and prosperity. The resulting fear of upsetting the applecart is shared not only by college students competing for fewer resources but also by their parents and grandparents in the rapidly graying baby boom, many of whom are facing unexpectedly austere retirements. Rancorous debates over political issues such as taxation and health care make clear that this huge, vocal population of seniors—generally a more neophobic, conservative group—wields increasing influence in national affairs, if only because they're the likeliest to vote. All of these social influences contribute to a newly fretful America that's wary of original ideas that have uncertain outcomes, much less of active problem finding.

The political system's short-term, election-cycle worldview only aggravates society's currently neophobic climate. A long-term, big-picture, innovative approach to, say, the energy crisis will be far less popular in a campaign than easy-to-grasp solutions that produce quick results: "Drill, baby, drill!" Reflecting on this pervasive shortsightedness at the national level, creativity researcher Mark Runco says, "Who saw our financial and energy crises coming? Maybe a few people did, but because of this conflict with the system, they could not keep us from falling off the cliff into wars, economic depression, and environmental catastrophe."

LIKE THE AGRICULTURAL age's plow and the industrial age's steam engine, the information age's electronics have changed the human experience as previous generations have known it. Just as we once focused our neophilia on advancing the ways of life enabled by farming, and then by powerful machines that mass-produced goods, we're now concentrating it on processing and organizing all kinds of electronic data that have become the foundations of our work and play. Like the upheavals that preceded it, this revolution is already propelling us into the next phase of our cultural if not quasibiological evolution. If we're to make the best use of our neophilia in a new epoch of endless novelty, we must make conscious decisions to ensure that it's working for us, rather than the other way around. In this regard, our relationship with our clever machines deserves special consideration.

PART THREE

# Neophilia Today

*Nine*

# The Really New Age

NO MATTER WHAT their specific chore, all of our smart electronic tools produce novelty. The seemingly daily advances in this dazzling neophilic technology, which show no signs of slowing down, have pushed us much deeper into the information age, which actually started back in the 1960s. Our nearly instant access to the latest world news, scientific breakthrough, music download, or cool TV show, as well as personal communications, has changed human life as certainly as farming and mass production and in many tremendously positive ways.

Bewitched by our steady stream of ever-niftier new gadgets, it's easy to forget that the information explosion began fifty years ago with the great expansion of radio and television.

Its next stage, known as the computer era, was kicked off in the 1980s by the proliferation of PCs and the growth of the Internet. Then the 1990s ushered in the ongoing digital phase, with its huge, high-def TVs and small, multitasking phones and laptops.

Our new information machines represent a major technological advance over the analog equipment that preceded them, which electronically recorded the waveforms of sounds or sights just as they are. Instead, digital technology translates those audio or visual signals into a binary code that represents the information in a series of ones and zeros. Then a device such as a phone or TV reassembles the numerical code into the original analog signal. The benefits include superior clarity, easy and inexpensive duplication, the ability to move among various media, and the high-density storage of vast amounts of data—a crucial element for ever-tinier yet more sophisticated machines with more functions.

From its beginnings, the information age has been about better, easier access to more and more kinds of data all day long and wherever we go. According to UC San Diego's appropriately named How Much Information (HMI) project, we now consume about 100,000 words each day from various media. That's a whopping 350 percent increase, measured in bytes, over what we crunched back in 1980. You may feel that you've been getting swamped only recently, but this growth has been surprisingly slow and steady since the 1960s: a 2 percent to 3 percent per annum increase in information per person when measured in words processed, or a 5 percent jump in bytes. As the HMI project's director, Roger Bohn, says, "There has been no sudden point when you could say, 'Oh my gosh! *This* is when it all started!'"

So be it, but even a seemingly modest 5 percent annual increase in bytes has a doubling time of about fourteen years, so that in just the past twenty-eight years, the amount of data we handle has quadrupled. This is a huge, if gradual, change by any measure, not least because, as Bohn points out, "we're dealing with four times more information with the same old biology on our end."

Technologists may now prefer to talk about "interruption overload" or "information pollution" or "fatigue," but *information overload* was originally coined in the 1960s in response to what back then seemed like a tsunami of TV and radio programming. The Internet notwithstanding, Bohn still regards these "old" media as the information age's major sea changes, and they continue to provide a surprising amount of our novelty. Nielsen research shows that Americans log nearly five hours of TV daily (however, many of those polled are elderly, and younger people watch much less real-time television). Listening to the radio comes in second, at a little more than two hours, followed by computing (just under two hours), video gaming (an hour), and reading (thirty-six minutes). The HMI project counts each medium separately, but these activities often occur simultaneously, as in gaming while the TV or radio is playing.

THE INFORMATION AGE may not be brand-new, but the digital revolution that churns out fresh novelty machines before you've mastered the last ones you bought has taken it to a new level. A global game changer, this technology is to our culture of data freaks what the bow, plow, and steam engine were to those who came before us.

These smart tools' most obvious benefit is that they enable us to use our neophilia to learn just about anything we want to, from fashion tips to the wisdom of the ages. A few keystrokes now unlock the gates to arcane information once restricted to certain haute professionals or yellowing documents in library stacks. Our choices of appliances and travel packages, to say nothing of colleges and chemotherapies, are much better informed than they were a mere decade ago. Whether you're rich or poor, black or white, male or female, young or old, expert or beginner, the answer to your question is as close as the nearest computer—a truly democratizing force that's apparent in any public library, where books are steadily losing shelf space to electronic media.

It's hard to overstate information technology's potential for helping you to delve into any interest, whether anime or Dostoyevsky. There's a lot of griping about TMI and ADD, but anthropologist Robert Kozinets suspects that most of it pertains to the workplace, where a person might indeed feel overwhelmed by unwelcome rings, pings, and flashing lights. "It's almost as if we live in two worlds," he says, "because in our leisure time, we're more and more focused." His favorite example is the striking expansion of fandom.

Not so long ago, sports fanatics and celebrity groupies had to wait for daily papers and weekly magazines to get the latest news about and photos of their favorite teams and stars. Now they can revel in almost instantaneous information about the

Nets and Jets, Sarah Palin and Brad Pitt. These familiar types of fans have been joined by a new sort who focus on a certain piece of the entertainment culture—*Mad Men,* say, or indie rock. Devotees of *Lost* even inaugurated Lostpedia, an online site that explores the show's complexities and invites social interaction as well as personal investment. Whether your taste runs to TV shows or Trollope novels, thanks to the Internet, as Kozinets says, "you can now go very deep into your fandom."

In addition to helping us learn, expanding cyber access, coupled with eminently portable laptops and smartphones, liberates us from many traditional categories and constraints. The old boundaries between the home, say, and the workplace or school grow fuzzier by the day. Some forty-five million Americans already take advantage of the fact that their jobs barely require an old-fashioned desk, much less a dedicated office or building, and do at least some of their work at home or on the fly. Not least because it relieves traffic congestion in metro areas, even the federal government increasingly allows employees to telecommute.

We use the Internet not only to work at home but also to enjoy and edify ourselves. During 2009, forty-seven million Americans watched or listened to music, dance, or drama online at least once per week. The plethora of blogs and Web sites like YouTube and Amazon help to blur the lines between professionals and amateurs by enabling anyone to contribute to as well as consume culture. About 15 percent of Americans now engage in serious photography, videography, or filmmaking, and like aspiring musician Antoine Dodson (whose furious rhythmic online challenge to his sister's attacker quickly inspired nightclub, marching band, and ring-tone variations), can present their work on the Web instead of more conventional venues.

Now that the Internet provides so much art for free, many writers, musicians, and other creative people worry about their financial survival, as do the flagging industries that formerly supported at least some of them. Rather than seeing artists as an endangered species, however, marketing guru Seth Godin says, "They're the only people who are going to make money ten years from now, because the way you make money is from your ideas." Shepard Fairey earns millions each year, for example, even though his art is free—unless you want a signed, limited-edition piece or an image to put on a corporate T-shirt. Those cost a lot, says Godin, "but the only reason people pay is because his free ideas are everywhere." Similarly, although the music business is ailing, "music itself is better than ever, with more being made and listened to. The digital thing took away the gatekeeper and the requirement that you need an orchestra to write a symphony."

Artists aren't the only original thinkers who'll prosper as the information age unfolds. Research that MIT's innovation expert Eric von Hippel conducted over a three-year period in England showed that, often aided by fellow enthusiasts on the Internet, individual consumers spent twice as much money as British companies on inventing new products and tweaking existing ones, particularly scientific tools and sports equipment. In a creative response to their generation's disastrously high unemployment rate, an eclectic group of twentysomething millionaires who founded their own Internet businesses recently formed the nonprofit Young Entrepreneur Council, which advises peers on how to start up their own companies instead of waiting around for traditional jobs.

That so much analytical, spreadsheet-type work has already been automated or exported to nations that offer cheap labor seems scary, but some forecasters see the closing of one door as the opening of another. Workplace savant Daniel Pink believes that the best careers in affluent societies will call for what he calls right-brained creativity, which is harder to outsource or reduce than logical left-brain skills. When there's a high level of material well-being, he says, "there's also a premium on iterating something new. Those novelty-oriented, right-brain abilities, such as artistry, design, and big-picture thinking, are the things that will matter most." Then too, in a historical blink of the eye, the Internet has changed the way business is conducted and created entirely new kinds of jobs, as exemplified by Google. Looking ahead twenty years, Pink predicts that his three young children will work in industries that don't even exist now, doing jobs that we don't yet have the vocabulary to describe: "After all, twelve years ago, no one could have said, 'This little girl here is going to grow up to be a search engine optimizer.'"

Information technology keeps us in touch with our friends and colleagues, of course, but it has also literally and figuratively given us a new way to see the rest of the world. The planet's 4.5 billion cell phones, many with cameras, provide live, you-are-there coverage of important but once inaccessible events, from revolutions in the Middle East to oil spills polluting pristine waters. These tools also make it easier to extend a helping hand to utter strangers, as demonstrated by the outpourings of immediate, electronics-enabled financial support for the victims of natural disasters.

Our smart tools also pull us together in new kinds of communities oriented around important issues. Whether your views align with those of MoveOn.org, NoLabels.org, or TeaParty Patriots.org, you know that the Internet is a powerful tool for effecting social change, including influencing election outcomes. Consumers are still "pretty voiceless" regarding important, potentially bipartisan issues such as energy independence, says Kozinets, but the Internet could help change that on a daily, grassroots level. "Why do ten houses need ten lawn mowers or snow blowers?" he says. "We could easily figure out systems to share and do with much less. That's still a very un-American attitude, so for now, the big questions are 'What's the halfway point? How could we move toward that? And can we start on the Net?'"

Historically, innovation has peaked when a Renaissance-style confluence of cultural currents—economics, science, religion, scholarship, art—promotes original thinking from diverse perspectives and collaboration on solving shared problems. It's hard to imagine a better tool for this purpose than the Internet, which can enable groups of us to produce better, smarter results than any one of us could achieve alone. The notion of "collective intelligence" first surfaced in the early twentieth century, when entomologist William Wheeler observed that a colony of ants could cooperatively act as a "superorganism." The term has gone through many iterations but now mostly refers to the cognitive surge that occurs when people and their computers are connected to one another. Instead of just thinking singly, or neuron to neuron, we can cogitate as a hive, or brain to brain. In a pop example, USC media scholar Henry Jenkins found that *Survivor*'s fans could predict the show's winners by posting many little clues online, some seemingly unimportant on their own, and piecing them together—a feat that no one person could have accomplished. Certainly no individual could sustain Wikipedia. After Kozinets invented netnography, a method for doing ethnography online, he wrote about it on the site. Soon, he says good-naturedly, "some bachelor-degree student in Minnesota started writing over my stuff, and now it's *his* stuff there."

Perhaps digital technology's least remarked benefit is that it reduces our carbon footprint by nudging us further from an industrial economy toward one based on information. Despite claims that computers soak up all our electricity, Bohn stresses that the actual figure is only 2 percent to 3 percent of the total we use. "From social networking to the buying and selling of virtual trinkets—that's where we want to be heading if we don't want to keep increasing our energy output," he says. "Some companies now pitch certain products as having a low impact on the environment, but most still haven't figured out that information products have the least impact of all."

THE NOVELTY MACHINES that can help us focus our neophilia on educating, liberating, inspiring, connecting, and greening us as individuals are also transforming our society. One stunning example is the expansion in the way in which we think of culture: the whole shebang of shared knowledge, beliefs, and behavior manifested in our arts, entertainment, cuisine, clothing, sports, music, and mass media, from newspapers to the Internet. In what some critics view as a society ever more superficial, changeable, and novelty-obsessed, anthropologist Grant McCracken sees a tumultuous yet vibrant work in progress in which the old modifiers of "high" and "low" no longer apply. In the past ten to fifteen years, he says, "we've dropped the 'popular' in 'popular culture.' Now it's just culture."

Many neophiles and neophiliacs have adapted to the digital era's nonchalant disregard for categorizing information as serious or trivial, art or entertainment. "They've adjusted to the turbulence and sheer dynamism of our world by learning to surf its commotion," says McCracken. "They've made a virtue of that necessity, taken on the literacy and skills to manage it, and get real pleasure from it. Others haven't." One result of this shift in attitudes about what constitutes culture is what he calls "a great intellectual flourishing outside the academic world, created by people who are just smart, clear, and mobile in ways that most academics are not."

Age is the most obvious explanation for the divide between the new cultural neophilia and neophobia. As an experiment, the Canadian McCracken consulted Facebook in search of important players in Toronto's cultural scene of twenty years ago and found that almost none were represented, and he sees the same generational disdain for or ignorance of new media elsewhere. Recalling a young newspaper reporter who was hired to cover the wired world but soon left the job because his older bosses just didn't get the importance of his beat, McCracken laments his fellow baby boomers' tendency to treat popular culture as "a dirty secret."

Back when the seventy-five million boomers were young, much popular entertainment was still seriously dumbed down to accommodate a less educated and media-savvy population. Sitcoms had laugh tracks to help viewers figure out what was funny. Movies were padded with interminable car chases, battle scenes, and the like to provide rest breaks for audiences struggling to catch up with the plot. These gimmicks, plus simplistic story lines and characters, earned the contempt of academics and intellectuals, who duly declared popular culture to be a wasteland.

Generation X challenged that smug view with an entirely different perspective on pop culture. Instead of disparaging it, says McCracken, "these kids said, 'No, this is our world.'" This hipper audience didn't need laugh tracks or car chases and wanted—and got—much more sophisticated entertainment. Their demand for quality TV encouraged more talented creators, such as the young writer-producer-directors Joss Whedon of *Buffy* and *Glee* and J. J. Abrams of *Lost* (both of whom come from industry families), to take the medium seriously. "When Gen X decided that popular culture could be interesting and fun—and profitable—that drew real artists," he says. "All this talent hits the jet stream, and bang! You get stuff that's remarkably better." One reason why *The Sopranos, Justified,* and *Boardwalk Empire* are far more complex than *Ozzie & Harriet, Gunsmoke,* and *The*

*Untouchables* is that "we no longer need those wee holidays to catch our breath. We can get it in one."

Generation Y takes Gen X's tech savvy a step further. As McCracken says, "These kids are so good at media that they don't have any of that hesitation of 'Oh, this isn't something I can afford to take seriously. It's not high culture.' They gave up that ambivalence and embrace pop culture as culture, which makes a big difference in your life."

A surprising number of works from that expansive culture not only entertain us more intelligently but also offer the kind of spiritual and philosophical uplift traditionally supplied by high art and religion. Hugely successful films such as *Avatar, Lord of the Rings,* and the Harry Potter tales are full of bits of ancient wisdom, psychology, sociology, and theology. Their fans, like those of pithier TV shows like *Battlestar Galactica* and *The Simpsons,* aren't interested in just sex and violence but also in existential and moral questions, the future, technology, the relationship between science and religion, and other weighty matters. Such entertainments have become myths and sagas that, like the Bible and the Bhagavad Gita, help people grapple with big issues, life's meaning included. "From one perspective, Cain and Abel is just a story, too," says Kozinets, who studied *Star Trek* fans for his doctoral dissertation. "It's what you do with the story that matters. Are people finding value in traditional religion or neighborhood associations the way they used to? They're not. In the Middle Ages, the church had the power and the deep stories. Now they're provided by popular culture—by entertainment companies and marketers—and that's what people are sharing reflections about online. The Net can also give you a voice in what happens to a story as it gets reworked, which is fascinating."

SOME OF OUR more complex, fast-paced entertainments help us figure out our more complex, fast-paced lives by providing new information on how other people cope—or not—with the human condition. In the popular fascination with how the rich and famous handle marriage and adultery, obesity and anorexia, McCracken sees our desire to "audition the change" instead of trying it at home. "By serving as vehicles of self-transformation," he says, "the stars allow us to watch others explore life's options almost like they were in a laboratory. They change themselves so that we don't have to." The Air Force puts an *X* before the names of its experimental aircraft, such as the X-15 fighter jet, and McCracken thinks that Lindsay Lohan deserves one, too. "She's an experimental creature who becomes a kind of object lesson in transformational activity. Celebrities who put themselves in harm's way on the screen and in real life canvas the options for us, which is why we care about them."

The relatively recent phenomenon of reality TV means that traditional stars are no longer the only public figures who can satisfy our neophilic desire to learn about how the other half lives. This unscripted form of entertainment featuring real people in real-life situations, which Syracuse University media scholar Robert Thompson unabashedly calls "a fascinating new way to tell a story that's more original than any since the novel," gives a high-tech spin to the voyeurism that has been an adaptive advantage throughout our evolution. "If you were curious about what your neighbor was doing, you might learn something that helped you to reproduce at a greater rate than others," he says. "I suspect, too, that the Neanderthals also got a good laugh from peeking into others' caves." Like McCracken, he isn't particularly interested in distinctions between high and pop culture. "Yes, we need to know about politics and art," he says, "but if we don't also know about love songs, recipes, and lawn ornaments, we won't really know who we are. If you scratch the surface of the common everyday things hard enough, the secrets of the universe will spill out."

Just watching a bunch of people going about their lives is generally a slow-moving business at best. What modern reality TV supplies that early documentaries such as *Nanook of the North* (1922) and *An American Family* (1973) didn't is a titillating element of contrivance that makes the new programs much more interesting. (Psychiatrist Robert Cloninger suspects that the manipulation extends to the careful choice of certain characters: "I find it hard to regard most people appearing in the shows as role models or representatives of the general population. I suspect that many of them have personality disorders or are extreme novelty seekers.") The groundbreaking *The Real World* (1992) treated its subjects like guinea pigs who were set down in an artificial situation that was deliberately designed to produce behavioral fireworks. People who were selected to interact in exciting ways and who otherwise never would have ended up together were plopped down in a house in a strange city. Then, says Thompson, "the directors turned on the cameras and watched what happened. Needless to say, it was action-packed—as much a chemistry experiment as a TV show." Hastened by big improvements in less intrusive camera technology, what Thompson calls "this dramaturgical Pandora's box" reached a new pinnacle of popularity with *Survivor* (2000).

Dating and courtship programs are vivid examples of how reality shows can engage our neophilia and allow us to explore and experiment with important life situations at a safe remove. Before the likes of *The Bachelor* and *Temptation Island*, says Thompson, our insight into what actually went on when people were romantically interested in each other was limited to personal experience and the secondhand, furtive, and limited information gained from friends' reports, overheard comments, steamy novels, and scripted movies. As much as he enjoyed *Sleepless in Seattle* and *You've Got Mail*, he says, "those films are to real relationships what a Greek temple is to a ranch house. *The Bachelor* was that suburban house, which offered street-level, functional, everyday information about relationships. Suddenly, you could watch real people engage in the seductive dance that courtship is all about. 'They're so insecure, paranoid, stupid, petty!' you think. 'They say the wrong things. Wow, this is really familiar!'"

THE CURRENT PHASE of the information age has brought us many tremendous benefits. Because it gives us the power to implement what we want to do and be more effective, Esther Dyson says that "if you believe people are generally good, then you have to believe the Internet is good, too." Offering one example, she says that the Long Now Foundation supplies an online forum for individuals eager to think together about the future in terms of ten thousand years rather than the latest trend. She illustrates the difference between these perspectives with a little story about three workers: "When someone stops to ask them what they're doing, one guy says, 'I'm laying bricks.' Another says, 'I'm building a cathedral.' The third says, 'I'm honoring God.'"

Society evolves in unplanned ways, and the ongoing digital revolution is still gathering steam. (In response to some ribbing about the occasional mistakes made by Watson, the IBM computer that trounced human competitors on the quiz show *Jeopardy* in 2011, one of its programmers huffily said, "Give him six months!") Some of its advantages and drawbacks are already clear, but others elude facile judgment.

Back in the 1980s, a good decade before ubiquitous PCs and Internet use, two brilliant psychologists—both intellectual celebrities in the sixties who ended up for very different reasons outside their profession's pale—made some prescient predictions about how the smart new machines would affect the human experience. An early technophile as well as a neophiliac, Timothy Leary predicted that soon computers would supply us with something called "virtual reality" that would make life so interesting that fewer people would bother with psychedelic drugs.

John Calhoun, who was best known for his theory that

urbanized crowding led to the dysfunctional ways of the "behavioral sink," was less sanguine about information technology. The dense populations of modern America's metropolitan way of life increased ideas, information, communication, and creativity, he said, but also the number of social roles we have to play, as well as competition, negative encounters, and dissatisfaction with daily experience. "Everything is coming at us faster and faster," he said, "yet we can't even learn from our experiences unless we have refractory periods to digest them in."

To cope with this overload of new stimuli, Calhoun predicted that we'd have to grow "more impersonal" in our dealings with others and increasingly dependent on computers to "help us preserve order and complexity and keep us from disintegrating into chaos." Sighing at his own lack of grandkids despite his several adult offspring, he said, "These machines make life so interesting that many people would rather concentrate on information than on raising children."

Decades before smartphones and tablet computers, these two psychologists saw that our increasingly sophisticated novelty machines would become so compelling that our lives would change in important ways that aren't always easy to envision or evaluate. Perhaps your fixation on your e-mail pings or your BlackBerry's blinking light sometimes brings to mind those experiments in which rats push levers to self-administer cocaine until death. Maybe you notice that your level of involvement with your gadgets is an eerily accurate gauge of your mental health du jour. You might vacillate between worrying about spending too much time online and worrying that when off-line you're missing something, between enthusiasm for your amazing tools and fear of being hooked on them. In short, it seems that as the amount of new information coming at you increases, so do your levels of both interest and anxiety—the approach-avoidance conflict par excellence.

# Ten

# Novelty Machines:
# For Better and Worse

As we live more and more online—learning and work-ing, buying and selling, communicating with others and entertaining ourselves—we neophiles can't imagine how we ever managed without our clever gadgets. On the other hand, there are moments when we wearily look up from our screens and think, *"This* is living?" Enjoying information tech-nology's advantages means making certain compromises with the human experience as we've known it that require careful cost-benefit analyses and behavioral adjustments.

Many of these trade-offs are variations on the "some-thing's gotta give" dilemma. The simplest one concerns a basic quality shared by all living things: responsiveness to the environment around you. As you know if you've had a run-in on the sidewalk or highway with someone who was engrossed in his or her wonder phone, you can't live in a screen and the real world at the same time. When you're focused on a glowing gizmo, you become like a research subject in an experiment on a fascinating phenomenon called "change blindness."

First, some inventive psychologists made a movie in which people passed a basketball back and forth in a gym; at a certain point, a large "gorilla" walked by this active group and even stopped to beat its chest. Next, the researchers showed their film to an audience whose members were asked to track the ball's movement and count the number of passes made. Some were told to watch the team wearing white shirts and others, the black shirts. The subjects focused so intently on their task that half of them didn't even notice the huge, incongruous ape. Moreover, viewers who tracked the white shirts were much likelier to miss the black gorilla. In other words, a staggering number of people were so engrossed in the task of monitoring a particular activity on the screen and so certain that they knew what was going on that they were blind even to an outlandish stimulus that should have been impossible to miss.

The change blindness phenomenon has profound implications for those of us who essentially live in various stimulating machines. The professional wit Fran Lebowitz sums up the problem when she attributes her success on the lecture circuit to her refusal to have a computer or a cell phone, which frees her to focus on and engage with real people in the real world. If you pass much of the day staring at your screens, you're going to miss much of what's going on around you, including at least one gorilla in the form of a valuable new idea, social exchange, or other opportunity. Electronics are often touted for enabling you to "be anywhere," but in reality that often translates to "nowhere."

Perhaps the most obvious something's-gotta-give conflict is that, like small children and pets, your e-mails, voice mails, texts, searches, tweets, links, alerts, and photos subtract time and attention that would otherwise go to other activities, including some that you claim to value more, such as doing your real job and hanging out with loved ones. Freud tells us that love and work are "all there is," but the technology that's good for the latter often serves the former less well. In a classic wag-the-dog scenario, the information machines that boost your efficiency can end up making efficiency your raison d'être. Unlike a text or Facebook posting, lunch with a friend or even a live phone conversation means all those inefficient expressions of interest—"How are you?" and "What's going on?"—that take up precious time that could be spent online or working! As *The Social Network* adroitly dramatized, the fact that Facebook was invented by an antisocial geek who tried to cheat his only friend is not a coincidence.

Free and easy e-access to everyone on the planet, including the pope and Queen Elizabeth, raises the question of what, if anything, such communications have to do with real interactions and relationships. It often seems that the more mechanized ways we have for connecting with others, the less time we actually spend with them. That the young people who sit silently texting each other in the same café are already the new normal raises many questions, including "Is communications technology improving communication or making it worse?"

The something's-gotta-give problems imposed by our new tools also contribute to the epidemic of what psychologists call the "time urgency syndrome." In addition to fostering the impression that there aren't enough hours in the day, says psychiatrist Robert Cloninger, smartphones and other gadgets "support the narcissistic idea that you're essential, and that you have to be in contact with others no matter where you are. It's very strange to see how that has changed our values about what information should be put into the public domain." The combination of electronically stoked feelings of self-importance and time urgency is even changing how we perceive time itself. Somehow, making a date for dinner or a meeting three weeks from now suddenly feels both uncomfortably constricting and impossibly remote. A clever essay about the near-futility of getting an RSVP in an era in which no one wants to plan more than a day ahead put it this way: "We prefer to remain flexy, solidifying our plans incrementally as the date approaches. *Let's talk tomorrow. I'll call you when I'm on the road.* . . . We're like the air traffic controllers of our own lives."

BEING ENTERTAINED is a good thing sometimes, but how about all of the time? One phone manufacturer hypes its product as an antidote to the few moments of "microboredom" that can set in when, God forbid, you're waiting in line or in transit. Nevertheless, a *Wall Street Journal* poll showed that a third of New York City's taxi passengers turn off the blabbering televisions now mounted in many cabs and 40 percent ignore them. Those disgruntled passengers, like the commuters who choose the train's "quiet car," apparently miss such brief, unprogrammed opportunities to think their thoughts and just *be*.

It may look like you're wasting time when you unplug from your gadgets and simply stare at the clouds or sit on a log, but gentle, effortless spells of reverie, or free-form musing and daydreaming, are crucial to your mind's healthy functioning and your productivity. The bottom line is that without these rest periods, particularly in our fast-forward world, your brain can't learn, remember, and integrate your thoughts and feelings properly. Restorative downtime allows you to drop your game face and sink into your innermost thoughts and feelings with no particular agenda. Your mind is liberated from the constraints—and gadgets—that tie you to the present: Where's that e-mail? Who's on call-waiting? You're free to roam through the past and future, reexperiencing the high moments from that ballet you saw last night or facing the fact that you're bored at work and need a change. Creative breakthroughs are also likelier when, relieved from rigidly focusing on tasks, you can wander into an original idea or a fresh perspective on an intractable problem, whose solution just seems to float into your awareness while you're gazing at the waves or walking home through the park. In fact, Cloninger compares the state to good psychotherapy, which he calls "almost a joint reverie shared between a patient and an empathetic therapist that enables them to make explicit what had been only internal." Interestingly, he finds that robust neophiles are apt to slip into this mellow mode more easily than highly structured people: "Novelty-seekers are more inter-ested in what is new or has changed than in organizing things."

Considering the shrinking opportunities for reverie in once quiet public places that now resound with droning CNN commentary and loud one-sided phone conversations, it's not so surprising that three different books on the value of silence appeared during a single month of 2010, or that one was drolly called *The Unwanted Sound of Everything We Want.* Even in private situations, technology can cut into our chances to simply be. The HMI project's Roger Bohn offers a personal example: He used to just think his thoughts on his long bike rides, but now he brings an iPod and listens to something. Speaking for many thoughtful observers of the way we live now, he says that except in the shower and for five minutes in the car, "I have very little time outside of my academic work when I'm just thinking. I speculate that it's not good for us to have no time to be in our own heads or to talk to other people without an agenda." His predigital youth acquainted him with reverie's pleasures and benefits, "but now, young people might never have that experience, so they won't know that they should try to find it."

Reverie was once a major part of childhood. The time that kids used to spend in the free-form worlds of imagination and the outdoors has been drastically reduced by television, com-puters, phones, and tightly scheduled activities. As a father of young children as well as a professor, Todd Kashdan, a psychologist at George Mason University who studies curi-osity, looks back on his own low-tech youth with something like wonder. In summer, he recalls, "we had no camps, programs, or internships. We had to figure out how to entertain ourselves on the streets and in our own little worlds." Tons of research shows that such free-wheeling play is vital to children's neurological, cognitive, and behavioral development, he says, "but their lives are now very structured into planned activities by parents who are basically chauffeurs."

THE GOOD NEWS is that new, unimaginably vast digital memory banks ensure that you can potentially remember everything. That's the bad news, too. For almost all of history, remembering has been much harder than forgetting, which is why, from our first writings and drawings to photography and sound recording, we have relied on technology to help us with the task. Suddenly, however, the digital revolution is reversing that natural order, so that it's increasingly easy to remember and hard to forget. The chagrined job applicants whose prospective employers access their goofy photos and anecdotes from social networking sites are merely among the first to experience the unintended consequences of data that can live on forever in cyberspace.

Despite the baby boomers' hyperconcern with Alzheimer's and aging's other depredations, forgetting usually isn't a medical symptom but a natural, highly adaptive behavior. If you couldn't do it, the truckloads of trivia that your brain processes and filters out each day would obscure the important stuff, rendering you dysfunctional. Forgetting also allows you to let go of the past, which is crucial to making decisions and getting on with your life. Citing that wise old maxim "Forgive and forget," Viktor Mayer-Schönberger, a professor of Internet governance at Oxford University who researches the drawbacks of limitless e-memory, describes a woman who eagerly anticipated a happy reunion with an old friend—that is, until nostalgia sent her to a file of their past e-mails, which rekindled a long-ago bitter rift. As he puts it, forgetting allows us to "unburden ourselves from the shackles of our past and to live in the present."

Imagine a not too distant time when to be alive is to be recorded: Heaven or hell? Since 1998, Microsoft's venerable wizard Gordon Bell has been his own guinea pig in an experiment called MyLifeBits. This effort, which seems as much an avant-garde artwork as a tech project, is a preliminary step toward "total recall," or the e-memory of an entire human life. To that end, Bell wears a small camera around his neck that takes a picture every thirty seconds and a device strapped on his arm that registers his biometrics. He records all phone calls, keeps all e-mails, and methodically scans and digitally stores everything from business documents to images of family heirlooms. His motivations run from the practical—a paperless life—to the sentimental—better family archives—but the most important are his desires for a superhuman memory and even what he calls "virtual immortality."

Leaving aside the question of whether having a boffo posthumous Web site means that you're not really dead, total recall offers some real advantages. First on the list is the ability to preserve every jot and tittle of history and learning.

Then, too, funneling stacks of moldering files and yellowing photos into a slim machine is efficient and aesthetically appealing, although the environmental benefits are still debated. Even Bell, however, is candid about the possible drawbacks and risks, notably the increased likelihood of being monitored by various Big Brothers as well as ripped off by credit-card criminals. Sending your complete health records to any doctor or hospital in an instant initially seems like a wonderful advantage, till you remember that those whom you might least wish to have that private information, such as prospective employers or insurers, could also find it easier to access. To retain e-memory's benefits and help to minimize its drawbacks, Mayer-Schönberger proposes "reintroducing forgetting" by giving electronic information an "expiration date," after which it's automatically deleted.

JUST AS WE may trade some benefits of forgetting for those of e-memory, we may agree to compromise the right to privacy for the convenience of life online. If Sir Francis Bacon was correct that "Knowledge is power," Google is nearly omnipotent. We hope the company really believes in its slogan of "Don't be evil," because it certainly knows some dodgy things about us that we've long forgotten, right down to that exhaustive search on bankruptcy or sexually transmitted diseases. We may think we get all that nice information for free, but we actually pay for it with something that we assume has no value: the search strings based on our queries. These seemingly innocuous data, which are the major source of Google's stupendous wealth, determine the online ads you see and also get aggregated with others' and sold for use in marketing. As Stanford University forecaster and Silicon Valley insider Paul Saffo says, in this new age of interactivity, "participation is mandatory. You have to put something in to get something out."

In a particularly chilling image, Mayer-Schönberger compares the online life to the Panopticon. The inmates of this ghastly prison, imagined by the eighteenth-century English philosopher Jeremy Bentham, were monitored invisibly, so they never knew whether they were being observed or not. As a result, they soon behaved as if they were constantly watched. Our ever more sophisticated technology ensures that more of our lives will be monitored in ever-subtler ways. Saffo predicts that software bots, which already scrape information for Google and screen applicants for certain jobs and mortgages, will perform many more such functions, with or without your awareness, much less consent. Phones and other devices will keep tabs on your location and broadcast it—not just to your friends but also to merchants who want to snare you as you walk by. Looking ahead, Saffo tips his hat to Richard Brautigan's prescience by citing his 1967 poem optimistically called "All Watched Over by Machines of Loving Grace."

Swapping privacy for participation in the online life exacts a social and sometimes tragic personal cost in the form of the frighteningly widespread disregard for what Supreme Court Justice Louis Brandeis wonderfully called "the right to be let alone." The Internet's relatively anonymous open mic, combined with Webspeak's brassy, sassy tone, encourages coarse, even cruel remarks that are broadcast to huge audiences with a single click. This electronics-enabled savagery is epitomized by but hardly limited to the cyber bullying that makes many young victims miserable and drives some into depression and even suicide.

Now that the loss or theft of your phone or laptop almost feels like a bodily assault, it seems only prudent to add the power to control your personal information to the list of basic human rights. Bell assumes that someday we'll be defended against cyber crooks and spies by universal encryption and the equivalent of Swiss banks for storing e-memories. However, as the WikiLeaks phenomenon so clearly demonstrates, even for presumably security-conscious governments, the careful, limited sharing of information that Bell optimistically envisions is contingent on some awfully big *ifs*.

YOUR NOVELTY MACHINES can deliver pretty much all the information you could ever dream of. On the other hand, that's far more than you want or could possibly use, which generates a peculiar kind of stress. This anxiety isn't new: Ancient scholars groused about trying to cope with the five hundred thousand scrolls in the library at Alexandria, and eighteenth-century readers clamored for the new compressed literary forms of the digest and "miscellany," or anthology. Nevertheless, electronic technology has taken information overload to a new order of magnitude.

Since first grade, you've been assured that learning stuff is good and that the more you know, the better off you'll be.

Now that the knowledge of the ages awaits you in that sleek little box on your desk, however, you might be wondering if maybe less is more. Voicing a lament shared by professionals in many fields, neuroscientist Michael Inzlicht says that his predecessors had to keep up with two or three journals, but he faces fifteen to twenty of them, not to mention his virtual stacks of e-mail laden with must-read attachments. Indeed, much of the digital era's information overload can be explained by the fact that in terms of time and energy, electronic messages are cheap and easy to write, copy, and send but costly to read and receive. As a result, says Inzlicht, "I fear my inbox every morning, which takes hours to clear out." Summoning thoughts of the change blindness experiment, he says, "Computers are unlimited, at least in terms of storage, but our mental capacities are finite. Once we cross a certain threshold, we get overloaded and start tuning out and missing good ideas and opportunities."

The pervasive sense of TMI not only derives from the visible amount that clogs your electronic inbox, including those promotions for Canadian drugs and penis-enlargement techniques, but also from the infinitely greater lode of information that you know is out there, lurking. An online search may seem focused and orderly compared with the overt distraction caused by ringing phones and e-mail *pings*, but those pages and pages of Google citations create a different sort of tension. TV and radio generated an overload effect when they expanded in the 1960s, says Bohn, "but there wasn't this sense of a vast sea of information out there that you had to carefully select from. Now that the Internet has put the whole world's library a few keystrokes away, you can search and perhaps find anything that you can think about, which causes anxiety."

Consider the task of staying informed of what's going on in the world. Not so long ago, this duty of an educated citizen required breezing through a daily paper and perhaps a half-hour of broadcast evening news. Now that multiple cable TV and radio channels plus Web sites provide round-the-clock coverage, staying abreast of current events is a Sisyphean effort. The survival of these media depends on fueling a voracious, neophiliac appetite for urgent updates on, well, everything, from air travel's latest indignities to who's leading in the Iowa polls a year before the election. *Politico.com* has been described as a site "where no detail is too small to report as long as it was reported there first" and whose young, underpaid, burnout-prone reporters put in long days trying to "eke out a fresh thought or be first to report even the smallest nugget of news—anything that will impress Google algorithms and draw readers their way." Observing that huge numbers of Americans who once got their news from Tom Brokaw or one of his judicious peers at least shared a certain experience, if not a point of view, media scholar Robert Thompson says that "that never has to happen now. We don't have to watch the evening news or the State of the Union or the Olympics, because we have seventy-five other choices."

Having lots of information about what's going on in the world is a wonderfully democratic force. Yet what empowers the voiceless and oppressed also provides a loudspeaker for once-obscure nutters and produces a sheer multiplicity of views that helps to balkanize the culture into angry, intoler-ant factions that won't pull together for the commonweal. As Thompson says, "The more blogs I read, the more I ques-tion the validity of a democratic republic." The Internet's next challenge is to reduce overload through more filtering and tailoring of content for particular users, which means that information will be edited down still further and packaged for particular demographic groups. As a result, like the fans of Fox and MSNBC, NPR and Rush Limbaugh, or the op-ed pages of the *New York Times* and the *Wall Street Journal*, we'll end up mostly hearing the opinions that jibe with what we already believe. As psychologist Barry Schwartz says, "We think that all this information makes us the masters of our fates, when in fact what we get is mediated by some entity. That's completely scary and a real concern."

Like the customized information we receive, the tools that deliver it can limit our social circles to those who have compat-ible gadgets and services. "Information overload forces peo-ple to decide what they will or won't do and to defend their choice on class grounds," says literary scholar Barbara Bene-dict. "Choosing to respond to Facebook, Twitter, or YouTube is a way of entering a cultural bubble that you've defined as better or more important than the rest of society. We're see-ing a culture breaking up into little groups that are defined by commodities."

UNPARALLELED ACCESS TO all kinds of new information, from vegan recipes to tips on reducing credit-card debt, can pave the royal road to self-improvement, but it also feeds the chronic dissatisfaction that accompanies too many opportunities and dispiriting comparisons. The vast constellation of home-improvement, cooking, and makeover TV shows and Web sites "really gets into who we are as Americans," says Thompson. "Our history is all about reinvention, about leaving the Old World for the New World and redefining ourselves. That's what the Pilgrims and later waves of immigrants did, and these shows just retell that tale. Oprah tells the same stories that William Bradford told in *On Plymouth Plantation*."

Rising phoenixlike from the ashes of your pre-makeover self sounds good, but constant exposure to the latest "ten best" lists and strategies for becoming smarter, thinner, younger, and richer can also breed discontent, guilt, and unrealistic aspirations. Esther Dyson contrasts our consumer society, in which access to nearly unlimited goods, services, and opportunities for self-improvement are just a click away, to Russia's very different culture, in which options and choices are limited. "People there expect to have a kind of crappy life. They try to make it better, but they don't feel so responsible for their problems. They're doing the best they can in a difficult situation. Here, if you're not successful and beautiful and well-informed, it's your own fault. You should have taken that course or done that makeover." Interestingly, she adds, the Internet has also caused a decline in hypocrisy, which also may be a mixed blessing: "Now that every famous person is revealed to have feet of clay, there's a lack of good role models."

Our information technology also multiplies our options,

whether for leisure pursuits or appliance purchases, to a degree that's sometimes way too much of a good thing for our neophilic species. After his extensive research on decision making, Schwartz says, "What I've learned is that we limit our choices badly." When we buy a gadget, for example, instead of prioritizing its usability, which is what really matters, we focus on its capability. Thus, we end up with the one whose tons of new esoteric functions cost more, make us anxious, and will never be used. Moreover, we never learn from these mistakes, he says: "We buy a digital camera we can't figure out, then we buy a smartphone we can't figure out." Illustrating the downside of too many choices where electronic data are concerned, he says, "Google has gotten us all the world's information, and we've seen that that's about as good as having none of it."

A shelf, if not a closet or garage, full of shopping errors is one thing, but difficulties with limiting more serious choices—of romantic partners, say, or career paths—is quite another. At first glance, a life of fewer possibilities may not seem appealing, "but what really enables us to exercise our freedom is having freedom within constraints," says Schwartz. "Many people found the old traditional norms too constraining, but the answer to too much constraint is not no constraint, which can produce a kind of endless distractibility."

GROUPS AS WELL AS individuals struggle with the trade-offs and approach-avoidance conflicts that arise from the combustion between the information age and our neophilic nature. At a

2010 convention of private-school principals, the main topic of conversation was the impact of the e-curriculum on education as we've previously known it. The headmasters had been pleasantly surprised by their students' success at doing computerized lessons at home during that long winter's many snow days. Such programming could also substantially reduce costs for schools, as well as appeal to parents and children eager to keep up with the latest thing.

On the other hand, the principals of these top-flight, competitive institutions were very concerned about jeopardizing education's nonacademic but vital dimensions, such as building students' character and social skills, and even providing good child care. They recalled how happy the kids had been to return to class when the roads were cleared. These educators had to consider a powerful new business model that could revolutionize both their profession and children's lives, but they were also worried about running the experiment with so little knowledge and understanding of the consequences.

The headmasters are hardly alone in feeling concerned and uncertain about the behavioral effects of the new technology that now provides so much of our novelty. Aside from some research on ADHD, multitasking, and other cognitive issues, the impact of the digital revolution that's already altering many other important aspects of our lives remains poorly studied. Over the past fifty years, however, there has been an increase in the incidence of all forms of anxiety and depression (except bipolar disorder, which is considered more "biological"). You can't help but wonder if the escalating amount of information we confront and the trade-offs we make to handle it might be one of the stressors that contribute to this dismal statistic.

The solutions to many concerns about electronic novelty seeking's effects on the quality of daily life come down to finding the right balance between different goals. In exchange for new information, you might surrender a certain amount of time and energy once spent on other pursuits. For greater efficiency, you could judiciously tweak your ideas about place, time, and relationship. You might trade some solitude for entertainment, privacy for convenience, or forgetting for electronic memory. A few problems, however, call for sterner measures on the personal and cultural level.

*Eleven*

# Caution Ahead: Silly, Unfocused, and Hooked?

A S INDIVIDUALS AND as a culture, we Western neophiles are inundated by torrents of information, much of it distinguished only by its novelty, that can lower our intellectual and emotional tone, distract us from important pursuits, and encourage compulsive behavior, even addiction. Aristotle said that a society should be judged on its capacities for productivity, pleasure, and contemplation. Our exciting machines offer great benefits where enterprise and entertainment are concerned, but their impact on profound thinking is more worrisome.

Electronic media are ideal for some kinds of work, but their speed, interactivity, and high degree of stimulation are not well suited to the slow processes of deep thought.

They supply information, not knowledge or meaning. Facts alone are not enough to establish real understanding, which requires context and reflection. Anyone who recalls spending a tough two hours parsing a few dense pages of a Philosophy I assignment knows firsthand that in addition to time, such demanding work requires considerable learning, as well as critical thinking and other skills that aren't inborn but must be laboriously developed. Yet as psychologist Barry Schwartz says, "The experience that comes from thinking hard for a while about a subject is no longer available to some people, because they don't stay on the task long enough to get to that point. Commitment has become a kind of dirty word, but there are a lot of things that, like playing the piano, only become interesting and fun after you commit and put a lot of work into them. You have to slog through the boring bits to become competent enough to have fun. Now there are too many new things that are fun right away."

The Internet's capacity for generating superficial novelty is epitomized by the meme: a cultural tidbit, from a catchy anecdote to a joke to an image, that spreads rapidly through society, now usually electronically. Some are amusing, creative, or informative, like the self-explanatory song called "United Breaks Guitars," which caused a brief but precipitous drop in the airline's stock. However, memes can also cause harm—as racist and misogynistic ones do—spread falsehoods, and waste time.

Consider Debrahlee Lorenzana, who was the meme of the week, and briefly an Internet celebrity, in June 2010. The curvaceous woman claimed she was fired by Citigroup for being too sexy and gorgeous and was duly inundated with attention from the media, which soon discovered that her ooh-la-la figure had been sculpted by plastic surgery, in hopes of advancing her goal of being on a reality TV show. Neither important nor true, this goofy meme was a fabricated piece of fluff whose sheer novelty—sacked for being too beautiful!—nonetheless attracted and squandered the attention of millions for days on end.

It's one thing to be silly and another to be destructive. "One thought in the mimetic community is that ideas are parasites that don't care what they do to their host as long as it helps them to spread," says marketer Seth Godin. "The Tea Party—or the Communist Party—is a political meme that doesn't care if it destroys the country, because its only job is to reproduce." Underscoring a major challenge for us neophiles in the digital era, he says, "The point is that novelty isn't necessarily good for us—it merely helps memes spread. That's why we have to muster focus and attention to fight against new things that would undermine our success."

Testing the assertion that the Internet's fountain of novelty for novelty's sake can undermine individual and collective contemplation by catering to our shallowest instincts is as easy as sampling the online vox populi. In addition to the BP oil spill and the World Cup, the top ten Internet searches of 2010 were Miley Cyrus, Kim Kardashian, Lady Gaga, the iPhone, Megan Fox, Justin Bieber, *American Idol*, and Britney Spears. On an arbitrarily chosen day in the spring of 2011, even the relatively lofty Wikipedia listed Elizabeth Taylor, Charlie Sheen, Lady Gaga, and Justin Bieber among its top seven hits. Observing that there are now eighty million blogs—and that the one featuring pictures of cats eating cheeseburgers has made a million dollars—Godin says, "If I put a list of top ten whatever's on mine, it will get twice the usual traffic. Something scatological or an attack on someone will also mean a dramatic increase." As to whether, all things considered, we're better off since the digital revolution vastly expanded the number of arousing novel stimuli we receive, he says drily, "I don't think we get to pick."

Junk information whose only value is novelty isn't good for you, journalism, or society. Much like Fritos or Cheez Doodles, the Internet's salty, crunchy, non-nutritious nibbles leave you unsatisfied and reaching for more. Even on a serious Web site, there's often little or no relationship, if not an inverse one, between an article's popularity—now often posted—and its importance. Anything about sex, celebrities, or pets can lead the hit list for days, obscuring the value of a major report on governance in Iraq or corruption in American banking. Not surprisingly, fewer publishers are "wasting money" on foreign bureaus and the long investigative pieces that keep the citizenry informed and the powerful in check, as the founding fathers envisioned.

Along with the sheer triviality of much of its material, the Internet's bullet-point, sound-bite style often compresses and oversimplifies important subjects to a degree that discourages serious reflection. Shakespeare tells us that "brevity is the soul of wit," but today it's less about bons mots than a tech-fueled, now-or-never impatience that's poorly suited to complicated matters. Successors of the digests and anthologies of yore, interactive Web sites, bristling with compartments and links that allow different levels of involvement, attempt to satisfy jittery, time-sensitive, overwhelmed readers who want their information new, now, and tight. Back in the not-so-very-olden days, forecaster Paul Saffo sought out a book or an article—at least a page—about a topic that interested him. Now, he says drolly, "I only need a haiku, so just give me a search string or a tweet."

But do we only need a tweet? Or rather, should we? An adrenalinized approach to information may suit newsbreaks, ads, and movie blurbs, but it can't do complexity, which leaves out an awful lot of the human experience. To say that Anna Karenina is "a cougar" or that Isabella Linton's problem was that Heathcliff was "just not that into her" says something but by no means everything about these complicated characters and their situations. Nevertheless, as Maryanne Wolf, a Tufts professor of child development who studies the "reading brain," put it, "Can you any longer read Henry James or George Eliot? Do you have the patience?"

Technology's way of undermining deep thinking was the focus of a much-remarked front-page story in the *New York Times*, titled "We Have Met the Enemy and He Is PowerPoint." The piece examined the consequences of the military's increasing dependence on the Microsoft program, which magically reduces the most complicated matters to wonderfully clear talking points and charts. Junior officers griped about the inordinate amount of time they spent in preparing the presentations, as well as the format's way of stifling discussion and criticism and muddling the decision-making process. As

Iraq veteran General H. R. McMaster put it, PowerPoint is "dangerous because it can create the illusion of understanding and the illusion of control. Some problems in the world are not bullet-izable."

Those likeliest to miss the general's point about the dangers of superficial thinking are students, whose brains as well as minds are still being modeled by their experience. Teachers and other thoughtful observers tend to say the same things about the young who set the technological trends that society will follow. First they express admiration for the kids' facility with gadgets. They allow that the Internet offers children who are interested in dinosaurs, say, or the Civil War all kinds of wonderful resources. Then they say that if a child has grown up online, however, he or she may not have developed the background knowledge and the critical and organizational abilities to evaluate all that information about Allosaurus or Nathan Bedford Forrest and select the best. They also worry that the online life's slick, sound-bite sensibility encourages a similar mentality. "The triviality, the desire for instant gratification—I really worry about that," says Esther Dyson. "Some young people are very bright and thoughtful, but there are more of them who surf life much more easily and don't stop to think."

Even on campus, the hope that our society, particularly its younger generation, can satisfy Aristotle's criterion of contemplation seems endangered by the enthrallment with electronic novelty. Original thinking arises from a foundation of serious learning, but college professors complain that the concept of research has contracted to the point that really good students go to the fourth or fifth page of a Google search, while most settle for the first one or two. Neuroscientist Jane Joseph is struck by the way in which some young people casually resort to plagiarism without realizing that it's a problem: "They just paste in something they got online as an answer on a test, then they say, 'What? That's wrong?'" Remarking on the steep decline in the quality of his students' writing over the past twenty-five years, media scholar Robert Thompson says that the young assume that Google is the fount of all wisdom as well as information, "but you can only get the knowledge most worth having on a deep human, not just practical, level if you go into a library and read books about things that have been thought and written about for a long time. There's a place for that, and I worry about its future."

Like the proverbial kids in the candy store, we neophiles confront an unlimited supply of new electronically produced goodies, and we need to think about our consumption of data in much the same way we think about food. A healthy information diet requires the self-control necessary to focus on the nutritious new things that have long-term value and ignore the junk that compromises our mental and emotional fitness. As Dyson says, empty Internet calories can play havoc with your "information metabolism" and interfere with your ability to think, but like greasy fries and supersized sodas, "the bad stuff doesn't force itself on us. We need discipline and better taste."

CONCERNS ABOUT THE intellectual and emotional coarsening caused by junk-food information are compounded by worries about digital technology's impact on our individual and collective capacity to concentrate. The caliber of your attention is important to the quality of your life for several reasons. First, the things that you focus on are the building blocks of your reality. Your brain figuratively photographs those particular subjects and objects and stores them in your mental album of the world, which means that they can affect your behavior. In a sense, what you don't focus on might as well not exist, at least for you. It's up to you to decide whether to construct your reality from the mental equivalent of bricks or straw. Practicing the piano or cruising discount shopping sites on the Web? Monitoring your old high-school classmates on Facebook or visiting a friend? Choice is all, not least because if you don't direct your "top-down," or voluntary, attention to a particular target, your involuntary "bottom-up" attention will choose one for you, homing in on whatever's most arousing in your milieu, no matter how worthless—and often on whatever happens to be new.

In addition to constructing your world, attention enables you to learn. If you want to absorb and remember something, you must first focus on it. If you don't, you won't, at least not well. The basic mechanics of attention explain why. Focusing is a process of selection. When you zero in on a particular sight or sound, thought or feeling, your brain enhances that target and suppresses other stimuli that could compete with it. In other words, attention is an either-or affair that allows you to home in on X or Y, but not both. Thus, when you try to divide your attention between, say, reading your latest text message and the speaker's remarks at a meeting, you won't fully recall what she just said any more than you'll remember the name of that stranger you met while looking over his shoulder for someone else.

Distraction is the enemy of learning. The possibility that the wired life could habituate the brain to states of high arousal and actually *train* it to flit between targets from texts to tweets rather than to focus, so that distractedness becomes a learned behavior or habit, is a legitimate fear. The most vulnerable group would be children, of course, both because learning is their job and because their experience is still literally molding their brains. The evidence suggests that they're devoting a lot of time and effort to becoming chronically scattered.

One study of sixteen- to eighteen-year-olds found that during their free time, they're engaged in an average of seven simultaneous tasks, such as texting, IMing, cruising Facebook, and watching TV, often at the expense of activities such as exercise, the enjoyment of nature, and interactions with real, live people. A large survey of media use, including TV, music, computers, video games, print, and movies, showed that eight- to eighteen-year-olds were thus occupied for an average of nearly eight hours per day, which doesn't leave much time for schoolwork. A study of four thousand teenagers found that 20 percent sent at least 120 texts per day, and 10 percent spent three or more hours on social network sites; the 4 percent of subjects who did both were twice as likely to smoke, binge drink, miss school, have suicidal thoughts, and be victims of cyber bullying. Research has shown that depressed people are likelier to log more hours online, but a large study of Chinese teenagers testifies that the reverse dynamic obtains as well. The 6 percent of the subjects who spent excessive time on the Internet—notably the fanatic, sleep-deprived gamers—were more than twice as likely as others to become severely depressed.

Even in college, where learning carries a steep price tag, professors must resort to banning and penalizing their students' use of gadgets during lectures. Envisioning today's twenty-year-olds in a decade or so, the HMI project's Roger Bohn says, "They're going to be much more fractionated than older generations are. They're constantly texting, even to someone in the same restaurant. That very immediate, rapid-feedback cycle has a seductive pull that leads people to do more of it, and I don't see anything that's going to put limits on that."

Much research on the impact of electronic information on attention understandably focuses on the still-developing young, but adults face many of the same problems, especially in the workplace. The volume of e-mails is such that some companies now hire special clerks who do nothing but screen, redirect, and delete them. Nathan Zeldes, who's an IT engineer at Intel, defines "infomania" as a mental state of continuous stress and distraction caused by the combination of message overload and incessant interruptions. His studies, like many others, show that this affliction exacts a high cost in both employees' productivity and their well-being.

The average knowledge worker gets three minutes to concentrate on any task before being interrupted by e-mail, phone calls, or other distractions and attends to most of them immediately. As in many companies, an Intel employee typically receives between fifty and one hundred work-related e-mails each day. Reading and responding to these messages and dealing with the extra chores they often entail significantly reduces the time and energy that workers can devote to their real jobs. Zeldes sums up infomania's impact by quoting the science-fiction writer Michael Crichton: "In the information society, nobody thinks. We expected to banish paper, but we actually banished thought."

Many of those distracted, stressed-out knowledge workers probably believe that they're boosting their efficiency by multitasking. Even a rudimentary understanding of attention's selective, this-or-that nature shows why trying to do two cognitive chores at once is doomed to failure. It's true that you can simultaneously perform certain tasks along with a rote function, as in unloading the dishwasher while chatting on the phone or sweeping the floor while listening to the news. In a famous experiment, psychologist Ulric Neisser even taught subjects to take dictation and read at the same time; however, they acquired the skill only with enormous effort and much intensive drilling and could apply it only to those specific activities. In real life, the trouble with multitasking sets in when you try to do two or more *demanding* things simultaneously, particularly those that tap the brain's language circuitry, as do reading, listening, thinking, and speaking. You experience the frustrating result of overloading this neural network whenever someone starts talking to you while you're trying to watch a movie or are on the phone. For the same reason, your efforts to read e-mails, say, when returning calls or listening to the news are prone toward glitches.

When you think you're multitasking, you're probably just "thrashing." (This evocative term is geekese for a situation in which competing computer processes spend so much time battling for access to a shared resource that little or nothing gets done.) Instead of doing two things at once, you're actually alternating rapidly between them, which ends up taking you longer and causing more errors. Rather than saying that Jane Doe is a good multitasker, it would be more accurate to call her a rapid switcher, and even the best of them will miss things and make mistakes. Hundreds of thousands of traffic accidents and many studies prove that phoning or texting behind the wheel, where you must focus on the road, aren't just inefficient but lethal.

Research has clearly established that multitasking is a myth, but many people can't accept the fact. They hope that just as weight-lifting reps build muscle, repeatedly trying to do two things at once will improve their cognitive fitness. It's true that your brain constantly rewires itself in response to your experience—indeed, that's what learning is. (After navigating London's maze of streets, taxi drivers—like med students during their training—actually increased the size of the hippocampus, which is important to memory and learning.) However, there's no evidence to support the wishful thinking that you can train your brain to focus on two or more cognitive chores at once. In fact, research conducted by Clifford Nass, a Stanford sociologist who studies our relationship to technology, and others shows that subjects who frequently try to multitask on different media do consistently *worse* in tests of attention than those who don't. Moreover, these distractible individuals are also more strongly biased toward

new information—the specialty of our novelty machines—
and have more trouble filtering out the unimportant sort.

ALL OF US succumb to the silliness and distractions generated by our information tools from time to time, but some
of us grapple with a more serious problem. You see them
everywhere, refusing to stop texting so the plane can pull
away from the gate, having loud private conversations in inap-
propriate public places, or gaming at the expense of real-life
activities—and, when they can't access their gadgets, exhibit-
ing the telltale signs of anxiety, discomfort, and distraction
that point to compulsion or worse.

Definitive research on whether the obsession with getting the latest tweet, text, or Facebook update qualifies as
an addiction has yet to be done, but many serious scientists
agree with neuroscientist Kent Berridge that the idea "rings
true." As a clinical psychiatrist as well as an expert on novelty
seeking, Cloninger goes further, unreservedly calling the compulsive use of electronics "an addiction." He recounts a recent
experience at the annual retreat of a group of high-powered
young superachievers, who were eager to learn how to relieve
stress. "We had some good sessions, in which I helped them
to get into states of relaxation," he says. "But the moment we
took a break, they'd tear off to a corner, turn on their phones,
and get back into their usual state of over excitement. They
actually *couldn't* turn it off." A little more than a decade into
the information age's digital phase, he says, "we've had a revolution, and we've already reached the point of saturation."

The compulsive behavior of these wired, wound-up masters of the universe suggests that tantalizing bits of new information can be, at least for some people, as enthralling as drugs. Addiction is mostly identified with chemicals, but it's quite possible to be hooked on certain experiences as well. Chances are that you, like most people, are dependent on something that adds a dopamine-doused zip to your life, be it shopping trips, tennis, or brain-teasing puzzles. Offering a benign example, neuroscientist David Zald says, "I'm a music addict." When he can't play his Chapman Stick, a guitarlike instrument with ten strings, he experiences mild withdrawal symptoms, such as irritability and "restless finger syndrome," in which he mimics playing. "Music isn't just something I want to do," he says. "It's something that I feel I *need* to do, so I consider it an addiction. It's not an unhealthy one, but it has an addictive quality to it."

As the tabloids make plain, some experiential compulsions are more problematic. Tiger Woods and Michael Douglas are among the celebrities known to have sought treatment for sexual addiction, and if Eliot Spitzer and Charlie Sheen didn't, perhaps they should have. The gambling problems of the moralist/politician William Bennett and former Louisiana governor Edwin Edwards have similarly been the stuff of scandals. (A large study of Parkinson's patients revealed that nine subjects became calamitous gamblers after being treated with high doses of drugs that activate dopamine receptors; when their medication was reduced, so was their disastrous risk taking.) Other extremes of dicey neophiliac behavior, from compulsive bargain hunting to a fanatic pursuit of life-threatening sports, haven't been rigorously studied, but many researchers think that they, too, can be addictions.

Alarming statistics on traffic accidents and deaths caused by "intextication" while driving offer strong support to the idea of an information addiction. According to the *Statistical Abstract of the United States: 2010,* between 2007 and 2008 alone, the number of texts nearly doubled to about 110 billion. One sign of being hooked is continuing to engage with a substance or experience despite the prospect of serious harm to yourself or others. Strict laws forbid the deadly practice of texting behind the wheel in many states and mandate tough jail terms for violators who hurt others, yet the urge is so potent that about half of drivers under the age of thirty are thought to indulge anyway. After her first bad accident and serious injuries, one teenager says she resolved to stop using her phone while driving, but within a year she had another crack-up: "I don't know—it's just so addicting. I just can't put it down."

All addictive substances and experiences provide rewards. Shots of new information could be exciting, like stimulants, or serve as anaesthetics that dull the psychic pain that can surface in an undistracted mind. Moreover, the most powerful rewards are randomly reinforced—that is, sometimes you get the payoff, but sometimes you don't. Dopamine's circuitry is especially responsive to pleasures that, like those of shopping, skiing, or checking your e-mail, aren't entirely predictable, which gives them a *frisson* of novelty. (The late, great pioneering neuroscientist Paul MacLean thought that orgasm's delight partly derives from the fact that your brain doesn't process certain aspects of the experience in a way that gets them "represented," or stored in your memory, which makes each event a bit of a surprise.) Conversely, too much of the same old good thing, whether lovebirds' 24-7 togetherness or an all-you-can-eat buffet, eventually blunts dopamine's stirring effect.

Like the casino, the Internet sometimes delivers a big payoff—you just never know when. From time to time among the solicitations for good causes, ads, and relatives' vacation photos, there will be some new information that's intensely exciting or beneficial. Those compelling news flashes and pieces of juicy gossip are like the coins that occasionally pour from a one-armed bandit. Just as you keep putting in your quarters, you keep rechecking your gadgets, hoping that this time, you'll hit the jackpot. As a psychologist, Paul Silvia is hyperaware of the invisible tentacles that drag people into electronic novelty seeking and refuses to get a BlackBerry or sign up for Facebook or Twitter: "I know I'd get obsessed, and that would be it. I really should get the Wi-Fi out of my house."

Just as most people are able to drink or play the horses within reasonable limits but others become hooked, it seems that most of us can use our information devices in a sensible fashion while some become obsessed. Research on drug addiction suggests that big individual variations in our dopamine systems and in *wanting* and *liking* could help explain why electronic cues affect us so differently. The transmitter's circuitry is not the only neurochemical system that's involved in addiction, but it affects the others, including the important opioid network, and is by far the best studied.

A dopaminergic *wanting* for cocaine, e-mail, or Grand

Theft Auto may be more instrumental in getting hooked than the actual rush of *liking*. Some drug addicts report that they enjoy their substance of choice a lot, which, as Berridge says, is at least a rational reason for partaking. Others, however, bring to mind those torch songs about a helpless passion for a no-good lover. Like certain reluctant shoplifters, guilt-ridden adulterers, and runners who can't cut back on their mileage despite painful injuries, these addicts describe a deep craving for something that they don't actually much like or enjoy but feel they must do. "They say that the pleasure they'll get is not worth the cost they pay," says Berridge, "but they can't help themselves."

The idea of wanting something that you don't like seems counterintuitive at first. "That surprised our lab, too," says Berridge, "but here's a way that it can happen." If you take some cocaine or amphetamine, the drug will trigger a burst of dopamine. If you repeat the dose twenty times in a binge-like, spaced-out sequence, however, the twentieth one will set off a much bigger release. Your dopamine system has been sensitized, or rendered hyperreactive, to the drug and will stay that way even after physical withdrawal from it. If you encounter a cue for the substance at a party after six months of not using, for example, you could still get a sensitized dopamine release. "You're not in withdrawal, so you don't have a need," says Berridge, "but you could have a very powerful want—even if you weren't expecting to like the drug."

Certain rats that are hyperactive, highly excited by novelty and inclined to take lots of drugs when possible, have particularly active dopamine systems, which get further revved up by cues for rewards. In a scenario constructed by Berridge, an information junkie with a similarly wired dopamine network would experience a surge of the transmitter and an arousing orienting response whenever he indulges in his habit. Because his *wanting* mechanism has learned to respond to new information as pleasurable, a cue such as a BlackBerry's flashing light or a "You've got mail!" prompt would create an instantaneous, potent desire—particularly in those who feel *wanting* without *liking*. Neuroimaging studies of such a person's brain done at that moment should verify his sensitized dopamine system's extra activation.

In drug abuse and perhaps bingeing on food, there's a point at which what has been a problematic behavior becomes an addiction, and a similar dynamic could obtain regarding novel information. As Berridge says, "A sensitized person who develops a very strong *wanting* without necessarily *liking* is past that threshold. The question is, 'If you're at the computer and getting that *ping, ping, ping*, how much pleasure are you feeling?' The people who want but don't really like the electronic stimulation would be the best subjects for research on addiction."

As we neophiles move forward into the information age, the unprecedented amount of novelty at our fingertips brings not only tremendous opportunities but also challenges, particularly triviality, lack of focus, and compulsive behavior. The first step toward maximizing the former and minimizing the latter is to understand the nuances of your own particular relationship to the new and different.

*Twelve*

# Navigating with
# Neophilia

LIKE SOCIABILITY, conscientiousness, or any other trait, your particular expression of neophilia has potential advantages and drawbacks. Exploiting its strengths and compensating for its limitations begins with an understanding of your characteristic responsiveness to new things, its role in your larger identity, and its impact on your goals and choices, which enables you to figure out the best strategy to make it all work for you. As psychiatrist Robert Cloninger says, "Every personality has its up and down sides. You have to know where your drives can function well or lead you into trouble, and that demands reason and self-government."

As with all behavior, neophilia has thresholds beyond which even a "good" tendency, whether a sense of adventure or a wariness of danger, becomes problematic. At one extreme, serious perturbations include crippling shyness and the apathy and anhedonia that can accompany depression and Alzheimer's disease; at the other, novelty seeking run amok can lead to calamitous risk taking or even be a symptom of bipolar disorder. "Swept away on a tidal wave of bliss over the new, manic people take on crazy hobbies and, say, get fourteen books on computational linguistics because it just sounds *so fascinating*," says psychologist Paul Silvia. "That kind of behavior is an illustration of interest's forward-looking, impulsive, obsessive side blown out of all proportion."

Milder manifestations of neophilia gone awry in either direction are far commoner. Hyper *approachers* who live to pursue the next big thing may end up with little to show for their shifting enthusiasms in terms of a stable career, relationships, or even sense of self. Incurious *avoiders* of novelty who passively wait for interesting things to happen can lead unnecessarily dull lives. Then too, some of us misjudge our own emotional responses to the new and different. Neuroscientist and psychiatrist Daniel Pine finds that in the lab, certain people who claim to be bold approachers react physiologically to novel stimuli like fearful avoiders, while some self-confessed neophobes who say they dread socializing or speaking in public do those very things with aplomb and show no metabolic indications of fear. Nevertheless, he says, "when you say to them, 'You sure didn't look like you were afraid,' they say, 'Well, I was terrified.'" Based on his results, he concludes that "we aren't movie cameras of our own lives. Our pictures of how we behave are reasonably accurate but also biased."

Most of us know, however, whether or not we roll out of bed in the morning eager for change and engagement with the new and different. Some of those who don't could enjoy more interesting lives by cultivating their neophilia, and some who do could benefit by learning to focus it better.

IF YOU TILT toward the neophobic end of the spectrum, you've experienced the discomfort of feeling worried, shy, or even overwhelmed in new situations. On the other hand, your sensitivity to risk also has clear benefits, starting with a better shot at a long life. Your quieter, more reflective nature also tends to be more empathetic and well suited to the worlds of science or the arts, where it's disproportionally represented by today's introverted Thomas Edisons and Agatha Christies. (The shy mystery writer suffered from severe stage fright, which led her to give up a promising career as a pianist for a quiet author's life.) Then, too, like the young Eleanor Roosevelt, naturally inhibited individuals who get the right support can learn to manage and even overcome much of their fearfulness. Indeed, some bold children grow up to have higher levels of anxiety, because they're drawn to the challenging fast lane. Neophobes may be likelier to be academics or accountants than astronauts, "but they keep things stable and in order," says personality researcher Marvin Zuckerman. "They don't mind routine, and they're less likely to divorce. It takes both types to make a society."

Not all of us are born with an active, searching approach to life, but that neophilic sensibility is something that can be developed. Even shy babies begin as original thinkers who have to figure out the world from scratch, but from fourth grade on, increasing social pressure to conform is apt to curb children's curiosity and unique perspectives. "If I ask you, 'Do you like growing as a person?' you're going to answer, 'Yes,'" says curiosity researcher Todd Kashdan. "But the real question is, 'In your daily life, do you stretch just beyond what you already know and do, or do you fall back on what's comfortable?'"

The first step in stretching your experiential boundaries is to override your brain's strong tendency to conserve energy by conducting business as usual. One of its favorite economies is to rely on familiar, sloppy but efficient categories and stereotypes: "I'm no good at sports/art/travel," say, or "That kind of person/activity/place has nothing to offer me." Kashdan suggests countering this lazy habit by "staying in the moment," because the mere act of focusing on the present will short-circuit your canned judgments. For example, he says, "you can decide that the next time you have a conversation, you're going to just listen for once and be really open to learning about the other person. It's hard."

Things that consistently give you pleasure are major obstacles to developing your neophilia. Predictable rewards— your favorite breakfast, the Friday dinner-and-a-movie date, ye olde holiday tradition—trap you into ruts and routines. If you're deciding what restaurant or beach resort to go to, your first thought might well be "Which place do I like best?" Opting for the sure thing, however, funnels you into the same experience you always have and closes the door to new possibilities. As Silvia says, "A reliable reward is a very subtle motivational trap that most people don't see, because they *will* enjoy themselves."

Instead of settling into your life's pleasant culs-de-sac, you can resolve in advance that the next time you plan a long weekend, watch TV, or go out to eat, you'll try a new locale, show, or restaurant—or at least, says Silvia, "order something new from the familiar menu." For the same reason, SUNY Stony Brook's influential marriage expert Arthur Aron suggests that long-term couples keep togetherness interesting by planning dates that are novel as well as enjoyable: ballroom dancing instead of seeing a play, say, or a trip to Canyon de Chelly instead of Cape Cod. Not coincidentally, he and his colleagues find that the happiest marriages are those in which the partners help each other to grow, change, and try new things.

Like cultivating your curiosity in general, developing a new interest in particular is guaranteed to improve your quality of life. First, however, you must figure out a pursuit that might appeal to you, which can be harder than it sounds. One of the most surprising findings from Mihaly Csikszentmihalyi's research on "flow" is that many of us don't enjoy this state of optimum, or peak, experience as frequently as we could simply because we don't know which activities are likeliest to produce it. As William James tells us, the utterly new is alien and incomprehensible, and the utterly old is boring. The endeavors that are apt to turn you on have just the right ratio of novelty to familiarity. Whether you incline toward flyfishing or studying the history of French furniture, the activity can't be something that you automatically get, says Silvia, "but you have to think that you'll be able to get it eventually. Interest leads to this really rewarding sense of 'Whoa! It's novel, but yeah, it somehow fits, and it will work.'"

Once you've selected a new pursuit, you face the challenges of overcoming your initial awkwardness and devoting time and effort to the learning that expertise requires. Even an earnest novice might at first compare abstract paintings to kindergartners' creations or modernist homes to shoe boxes or fishbowls, while the delighted connoisseur swoons. Beginners don't know enough about the subject yet, says Silvia, "so they have to struggle to get to getting it."

One way to limit the frustrations of the approach-avoidance conflict that often accompanies learning something new is to start small and keep it simple. "Everyone assumes that the way to make a pursuit interesting is to make it wild and different and complicated," Silvia says. "Try making it easier and more comprehensible instead." Before you rush out to buy lots of new equipment, for example, you might look over some basic books about carpentry or rock gardens and experiment and improvise with tools that you already have. Local, affordable, low-commitment continuing-ed classes offered by many community colleges are a great resource, he says. "They unleash all kinds of crazy passions for writing memoirs, scrapbooking, history. A good teacher really can make almost anything engrossing by showing the mystery—the novelty—of it in a way that you can understand."

Research on original thinking provides more good insights into how to use neophilia to make your life more interesting.

The term can sound elitist or airy-fairy, but you bring creativity down to earth whenever you rearrange the living room furniture just to have a change, tweak a classic recipe, figure out how to make a good relationship better, or contribute a new perspective to a political debate. As researcher Mark Runco says, "It's fine to be a conformist when you drive, but not when it's time to express yourself or question something." Even using little tricks to jack up your problem-solving skills, such as translating a challenge from words into pictures or finding analogies to it, enhances your capacity for original thinking. "When you change creative tactics," he says, "it's not just tactics that change."

A proven way to work more inventively in one area of interest is to delve into another. This "professional marginality" enabled the psychologist Daniel Kahneman to get the Nobel Prize in economics for finding behavioral flaws in decision making that myopic economists couldn't see. When biologist and science historian Robert Root-Bernstein, a MacArthur winner himself, interviewed other grantees, he found that far from being narrow specialists, they all had very wide interests that gave them fresh insights into their primary field. For the same horizon-expanding, border-crossing reasons, living abroad or learning a new language also helps you to see the same old world anew.

Creativity is romantically associated with the lone, misunderstood genius, but in reality, original thinking is often a collaborative effort. Music, especially jazz, is the classic example, but computer programming, filmmaking, product design, and many other fields also depend on cooperative brainstorming.

The grueling six-day regimen of producing comedy for *Saturday Night Live* begins each Monday with a problem-finding ideas meeting sans the traditional boardroom table. "It's more likely that we'll be lying on the floor, surrounded by candy wrappers," says twentysomething writer Simon Rich. He describes this creative group effort as "coming up with a thousand terrible ideas in the hope that one will be salvageable."

Once they find the week's concepts, various *SNL* staffers pitch in to develop about forty-five scenes, work up the best ones, then fine-tune them literally right up to airtime. Everyone from set designers to musicians contributes, says Rich, "and embarrassingly, the actors tend to be just as good at writing as the writers." Offering his own testimony to professional marginality, he says that although he also enjoys his other, solitary vocation of writing fiction, "I don't think I could do that twelve months a year. I'd get lonely."

Much of the experts' advice on how to become more curious, interested, and inventive comes down to "Just do it." Kashdan offers a romantic example: "If you see a beautiful stranger walking down the street wearing a T-shirt of your favorite eighties band, you're going to be intrigued, but the experience won't impact the quality of your life if you don't take action." Similarly, creativity researcher Robert Weisberg recalls a young woman who feared that she lacked special talent and resisted taking a studio art course until her school finally forced her to if she wanted to graduate. "The teachers showed her and the other kids what to do," he says, "and at the end of the year, the exhibit of their work was incredible. All you have to do is to want to do it!"

. . .

IF YOUR ATTITUDE toward novelty and change inclines toward the behavioral spectrum's neophiliac or even just *con brio* end, you contend with different behavioral issues than those faced by your more cautious brethren. Many activities that fall into the category of "new and interesting" can be questionable if not downright dangerous: drug experimentation, infidelity, risky sports, gambling, crime . . . The list goes on and on. An intense attraction to novelty can lead to "Why not learn to tango?" but also to "Why not try meth?"

Neophiliacs' lives may be riskier, but they can also be very productive—and in more than one sense. Along with the prudent and sensitive, society also needs the bold entrepreneurs who generate start-ups, the firemen who race into burning buildings, and the ER doctors who stay cool in bloody crises. Then, too, from an evolutionary standpoint, success lies in surviving to reproduce, and neophiliacs are well represented in the population. Because their sensation seeking extends to the boudoir, says Zuckerman, they "leave more genes behind— or they used to, before birth control!" From this evolutionary perspective, astronaut Story Musgrave would be a big winner even if he'd never set foot on the moon, simply because he has seven children, aged fifty to five years.

To channel neophilia's flared-nostril expression more skillfully, you must first stop using curiosity like a floodlight and start focusing it like a laser on the new things that promise long-term benefits. These worthwhile targets of your attention usually relate to something that you really care about, whether Buddhism, sailing, or a frail, elderly parent. It's not like we don't know that we should focus on important rather than trivial stuff. The problem is that daily life's hustle and bustle has a way of gradually obscuring or distracting us from our deeper goals and values, so that we can easily get snagged by exciting but ultimately worthless stimuli. Just taking time to re-identify your priorities and the subjects worth an investment of your finite interest is a productive exercise in itself. As Kashdan says, "Once you see the bigger picture of 'What do I want to do with this day, week, life?' it suddenly becomes a lot easier to resolve conflicts about where to invest your time at any given moment."

Managing a powerful attraction toward the new also requires developing a critical attitude about the value of novelty and change per se. Long-standing cultural traditions, from the great religions to the secular ideals of Yankee thrift or the hardworking pioneer and immigrant ethics, have historically drawn attention to enduring goals and long-term meaning. The weakening of those institutions and influences leaves many individuals to grapple alone with some very big questions, including, "Why stick with X if something— or someone—new and better comes along?" For example, the two major biological drives involved in relationships send very different messages about novelty. The bonding between spouses or infants and parents depends on familiarity. As the Coolidge effect makes plain, however, the flames of physical attraction are fanned by the new and different. The relaxation of traditional constraints on sex outside marriage have sent rates of wedlock and births within it plummeting, which has serious social as well as personal implications, particularly regarding the rapidly growing ranks of single mothers and their children.

Training a skeptical eye on novelty for novelty's sake is crucial regarding matters of fashion, which now extends far beyond its traditional limits of clothing and decor. To Paul Saffo, the best gauge of a gadget's style quotient is whether it's as useful to its owner when it's turned off as when it's on. "Under Steve Jobs," he says, "Apple is a fashion designer, and the iPhone and iPad are fashion statements. Once manufacturers can get us thinking in terms of style, they know we'll want something different, not the same old thing, which makes us more open to novelty." He may be a futurist, but Saffo still uses an old-fashioned paper calendar and an HP-41 calculator from the 1970s, because he finds them more useful than their unnecessarily complicated and costly replacements. Like a good-natured version of a woe-unto-ye prophet, he points to late Rome, prerevolutionary France, and eighteenth-century Portugal, warning that "all civilizations fail by turning everything into entertainment and fashion. We need to become more explicit and conscious of deciding to make something new, instead of just doing it because it's novel."

NEOPHOBES AND NEOPHILIACS have their special issues to deal with, but nearly all of us must contend with the most recent challenge to managing neophilia: floods of new information. When he speaks to different groups, Kashdan finds that he invariably faces the same question: "How can you say that curiosity is a good thing when I can't get off Wikipedia, the *New York Times*, the *Huffington Post,* and my other bookmarks, so that I accomplish nothing in the course of a workday?"

Complaints about drowning in digital data partly reflect the fact that we're still slogging through the time-honored process of getting used to the new ways things are. Socrates lamented that the crazy trend of literacy promoted intellectual laziness and endangered the venerable practices of memory, inquiry, and debate that led to real knowledge. Later scholars grumbled that the flood of books churned out by the printing press forced them to read too fast—and silently rather than aloud. Historical precedents notwithstanding, we really do need better techniques and tools to help us deal with our unprecedented storms of data. As media scholar Robert Thompson puts it, "The big human story at the turn of the twenty-first century is that we've moved from being a species desperately seeking stimulation and novelty to one that now needs to filter an infinite amount of it to get at what's most interesting. We've gone from being hunters and gatherers of information to being editors of it."

Our forebears invented graphs and charts to sort and simplify complex material, and we've come up with some similar electronic aids, notably computer programs that search for certain information, find us the best prices, and select things we might like. However, we need more sophisticated ways to separate the wheat from the chaff in the vast harvest of data. When we complain that there's nothing on TV, even though the average home has 120 cable channels, "that just says that the search function has gotten too hard," says information analyst Roger Bohn. "It's ludicrous to claim that there's nothing to watch, but not to say that there's nothing that you *know* that you want to watch."

Along with throwing more filtering technology at our information technology, we need to develop better social and personal strategies for managing it, starting with teaching the young how to use the new media and machines wisely, just as they're taught math and science. The first lesson should be moderation, says Thompson: "Doing anything too much, even reading, is a bad idea, and these gadgets can be like succubi. Before you know it, you can spend three hours online, which is time subtracted from other things and leaves you with that sense of self-loathing."

As individuals, we need to establish certain rules that prevent our novelty machines from choosing what we pay attention to, willy-nilly. In a classic older study that looked at the ratio between the amount of time that residents spent reading and the quantity of information that came into their homes, the determining factor was the number of TV channels: the more stations, the less reading, which is particularly sobering when you consider that back in the 1960s, the average home got twelve channels. In one simple example of how to control your technology rather than letting it control you, Shantanu Narayen, the CEO of Adobe, only responds to an e-mail if he's the sole addressee, replies quickly if at all, and then deletes it.

Worthless information is like empty calories, but it's hard not to nibble on the cognitive equivalent of buffalo wings, not least because of the ingrained idea that learning something new is a good thing per se. Then, too, if you log on to

MSNBC.com, eBay, Gawker, or any of the other thousands of Web sites and blogs, chances are that you *will* find something that arouses your curiosity. Once you start that impulsive clicking, however, whether you're checking out the latest on Angelina Jolie or Hillary Clinton, it's likely that you'll have little or nothing to show for your expenditure of time and energy afterward. The vast storehouse of trivial new data becomes what Silvia calls "a cruel trap that exploits our ability to be interested, because much of that electronic poking doesn't lead anywhere."

Borrowing an effective dieter's tool can help you control your appetite for junk information. People who jot down everything they eat in a simple notebook can end up consuming a third fewer calories each day. In the same way, keeping tabs on your time online—and its quality—can help curb that appetite. Your e-log might surprise you. When you're pressing keys, clicking on links, and watching the screen change, you feel like you're accomplishing something, but looking back, you might discover that often you didn't. You might also wonder why you're devoting several hours a day to texting and social networking when you maintain that your top priority in life is spending more time with loved ones, say, or securing that corner office.

The discipline of going on an information diet and monitoring the quality of your online life may cause you to question not only the premise that it's always productive but also the assumption that it's fun or cool. Your log might reveal that the actual experience is often disappointing and can generate that "lost weekend" feeling, complete with hangover. Kashdan posits that the dysphoria that often accompanies aimless Net browsing reflects the brain's frustration at being confronted with too much random information, so that it can't do its job of finding the big picture and producing that satisfying *Aha!* Paraphrasing the surprising realization that many people come to after keeping an e-log, he says: "Actually, I'm not happy when I'm going through the two hundred and fifty TV channels or searching on the Internet for two hours for the latest, most scintillating information that no one else knows about. I thought I was, but I'm not."

As is the case with food, moderation in consuming new information is harder for some of us than for others. We've all become upset when we can't access our data, which is by no means always a sign of being hooked, as neuroscientist Kent Berridge says: "There's also a more cognitive, rational drive for that response, in that all of us share the anxiety of just trying to keep up." However, for those who feel that their craving for information is out of control, addiction research offers some practical suggestions. *Wanting* is often short-lived, so Berridge recommends simple strategies that distance you from the sudden dopaminergic urge until it wanes. Before opening that e-mail or clicking on that link, for example, you could step back for a moment and count to ten or take some deep breaths. This pause both relieves the immediate desire's sharp intensity and forestalls a knee-jerk response, which allows you to decide calmly whether to pursue the information or not.

If such attempts at behavior modification fail, the next step for insatiable information bingers is to impose strict

schedules on their use of tempting technology. The unwilling-
ness or inability to set such limits and take time-outs from
electronic novelty seeking is itself a psychological feature of
addiction and will worsen the problem, because each shot
of new information feeds the appetite for more. The last
recourse, short of seeking professional help, is to try tools
such as apps that block Internet access for a certain number
of hours or disable drivers' phones. As Silvia puts it, "We
need that good old-fashioned behaviorism that says, 'It may
be hard to control your actions at times, but you can try to
control your environment and manipulate it in a way that
takes the choices out of your hands.'"


SOME PROFOUND INSIGHTS into how to make discriminating
decisions about which new things are worthwhile and which
aren't in the fast-paced twenty-first century come from a seemingly incongruous source: the plain-dressing, horse-and-buggy
Old Order Amish and Mennonite people. They're among the
most recognizable of the many Anabaptist groups who are descended from eighteenth-century refugees who fled to America
from Europe, where their preference for adult rather than
infant baptism subjected them to brutal persecution. This
distinctive Christian sect, which arose during the sixteenth-
century Reformation, is dedicated to practicing the simple,
humble life described in Jesus' Sermon on the Mount, which
begins "Blessed are the poor in spirit . . ."

The Old Order cultures are guided by their literal inter-
pretation of Saint Paul's stern advice to the first Christians:

"Be not conformed to this world." Accordingly, they dwell apart from the larger society in their own communities and converse in "Pennsylvania German." Their ideal is to live close to the land as farmers, and their children stop attending school after the eighth grade. Their society seems exotic to outsiders, yet its agrarian sensibility resembles that of much of rural America into the late nineteenth and early twentieth centuries and so offers a sense of how life used to be here not so very long ago.

The most striking way in which Old Order groups signify their nonconformity to modern society is their highly controlled, selective approach to novelty in general and technology in particular. The point, which outsiders often misunderstand, isn't that modern amenities from cars to dishwashers are considered sinful or immoral per se. Such things are forbidden because they would jeopardize this deeply spiritual culture's raison d'être: a simple, peaceful, earthy, contented way of life that centers on the group's well-being rather than that of the individual.

"Their basic question is, 'What will this technology do to our community? How would it change or shape us?'" says Donald B. Kraybill. He's a sociologist at Elizabethtown College in Lancaster County, Pennsylvania, where the Old Order groups abound and where he grew up on a Mennonite farm. "Their logic is that they want to keep people together. So they stick with horses, which can only travel so many miles per day, rather than go with the automobile, which promotes speed, mobility, and independence and would fragment their community by taking people away."

Their values-first mentality regarding novelty and change explains why some Old Order people will use batteries to power tools in their shops and safety lights on their buggies but refuse to tap into the public electricity grid. They believe that the convenience of flipping a switch for every little chore would undermine their simple, hands-on life. Similarly, TV, radio, and computers are not permitted, certainly in the home, although some communities allow businesses to use a special "neutered" computer that doesn't run video games or the Internet. Paraphrasing the rationale, Kraybill says, "'Why would we hook up to the cesspool of Hollywood and funnel that to our families? That would be stupid.'" Describing the Old Orders as "the polar opposite of the Twitter world," he says, "these people like grounded, organic, face-to-face communication in high-context settings. When they see a neighbor, they know his grandfather and granddaughter—his whole history."

You might assume that in high-tech twenty-first-century America, the Old Order population is a picturesque, quaint, dwindling minority whose young people desert in droves, but you would be wrong. In fact, this vibrant society now doubles every eighteen years and has spread from its roots in Lancaster County to some four hundred groups in twenty-eight states. About 90 percent of its children—there are usually six to eight per family—voluntarily seek baptism and join the church between eighteen and twenty-two years of age. Despite their greater exposure to the larger world these days, the young's rate of staying in the church has actually risen over the past twenty to thirty years. In contrast to many mainstream young adults trying to find themselves, says Kraybill, "these kids know who they are by the time they're twelve. They marry and have kids by nineteen or twenty and find great meaning in their extended family, which generates high levels of satisfaction."

Nothing is the way it used to be, and all cultures evolve to accommodate change. Their very success has compelled the Old Order groups to modify their way of life in significant respects. Agriculture remains the ideal occupation, but in Lancaster County a hundred-acre farm now costs $1.5 million, which puts the vocation out of reach for many offspring of big families. It's possible to start a carpentry shop or the like for $30,000 to $40,000, however, so now about 60 percent of workers are employed in small businesses such as furniture making, welding, manufacturing farm equipment, or construction. These days, says Kraybill, "a crew of Amish carpenters might travel to Princeton to install a $100,000 kitchen."

Recent decades have brought tremendous changes to Old Order domestic as well as economic life. Many fathers now work away from home, which means that for the first time, women are experiencing the industrial age's housewife role. In their traditional preindustrial families, men shared much of the labor, says Kraybill, "but now women are stuck at home alone with the kids. It's the subject of a big debate." Not coincidentally, 20 percent of Lancaster's small businesses, including greenhouses and quilt and dried-flower shops, are now owned and run by women whose children are older.

Changes notwithstanding, the Old Order groups cleave to the core of their demanding way of life because for them it successfully addresses very basic human questions of meaning, belonging, and identity. As Kraybill says, "They have a deep sense of contentment, rootedness, family, and community." Nothing better illustrates that feeling in action like a barn raising. "If yours burns down, men, women, and children rally round the disaster and build a new one in two days," he says. Despite all of the hard work involved, this highly democratic effort is also creative and fun, with lots of laughing and joking. "They all know that if their barn had burned, their friends and neighbors would have turned out for them. That deep sense of caring for the community that's exhibited in this ritual is the essence of who they are."

The Old Order's simple, agrarian lifestyle is not for everyone—successful converts are rare—yet their careful, thoughtful approach to the long-term consequences of novelty and change for values that they hold dear holds important lessons for mainstream society. "They're skeptical about 'progress,' and whether something new is really going to enhance life," says Kraybill. "They watch and observe for a while, checking it out, and if it works for them, as batteries do, they'll take it. But they don't just assume that new is better, as most other Americans do."

As WE MOVE into a future in which the only certainty is change, our neophilia remains one of our greatest assets. One day just after the attack on Pearl Harbor, young Abraham Maslow, who would become a father of positive psychology and prophet of the "peak experience," felt overcome by war's destructiveness and waste. To relieve his despair, he decided to study the most mentally healthy people he could find. He discovered that these "self-actualized" individuals, who had developed their full personal potential, shared certain qualities. They were outward looking, spontaneous, creative, willing to take on challenges, and open to new ideas, people, and things. In other words, they were vigorous, well-balanced neophiles.

Wide-ranging conversations with an eclectic group of behavioral scientists, anthropologists, technologists, and others interested in how we'll cope in a world of increasing novelty and change range from the practical to the seemingly fantastical. Some observers think that it's just a matter of time before we embark on a new kind of evolutionary development that involves some sort of meshing between bodies and machines. Brain chips may sound like science fiction, but serious research by MIT's robotics whiz Rodney Brooks and others, to say nothing of the many people already walking around glued to their gadgets, if not quasi-implanting them in their ears, suggests that the idea is not so far-fetched. As anthropologist Rick Potts says, "We evolved the brain's ability to take in, attend to, and sort information almost instantly, but filtering all of today's electronic data is hard. A symbiosis between our neural, cognitive networks and our electronic ones has already started."

The hopes of would-be multitaskers notwithstanding, the least likely prospect is that our stepped-up responsiveness to the deluge of new stimuli will cause a genetic change in the way the human brain is organized. As anthropologist Ian Tattersall puts it, "We can't expect genes or evolution to ride in on a white horse and rescue us." On the other hand, we're already launched into the neophilic process of learning how to adapt to increased information. "The human brain is a highly plastic organ whose development significantly depends on how you use it," he says. "We're still exploring the capacities of this organ that we've had for a very long time." In response to their unprecedented electronics exposure, for example, young people have raised their stimulation threshold to the point that capturing their attention may actually require the arousal from all those little compartments and flashing things on their screens that vex their elders. Indeed, the experience of processing more information has made all of us better at it, which has enlivened the whole culture. As Berridge says, "The brain is up to the task of plugging in to new stimuli and making them attractive, rewarding incentives. That's why, although we didn't evolve with computers, they're now able to turn us on and pull us out."

In short, at least for the time being, the best way to enhance your ability to handle novelty is to reconnect to neophilia's evolutionary purpose: to help you adapt to change and to learn about and create new things that matter, while dismissing the rest. In fact, much of the experts' advice on how best to live in a world of potentially limitless distractions can be distilled into two words: selectivity and balance. Observing that TV commercials now use novel stimuli to arouse our brains and snag our focus every five seconds—in effect, training us, especially the young, to be distractible—Cloninger says, "You're going to be confronted with many stimuli designed to grab your attention and addict you, so you should be very careful about what you expose yourself and your children to. Everyone needs time for quiet, reflection, and reverie. You have to achieve an equilibrium between those needs and other stimuli, or you'll have problems."

More than a century ago, the writer Gustave Flaubert offered an excellent reason for cultivating balance and discernment regarding change and the new: "Be regular and orderly in your life like a bourgeois, so that you may be violent and original in your work." Sounding this same economical note, creativity researcher Oshin Vartanian says that considering the brain's limited store of energy and active novelty seeking's high metabolic cost, you would do well to consider some questions before committing to something new, whether an idea or an object: "Why should I take this up if the set of scripts that I follow daily are doing a good job for me?" Where technology is concerned, he suggests asking, "Why exactly do I need another novelty-producing gadget? It will incur certain mental costs, so if I get one, where will those resources come from?"

The record of neophilia's role in our evolutionary past offers us valuable insights as we continue our age-old work of trying to survive and thrive in a changing world. Just as environmental events nearly extinguished us long ago in Africa—and continue to exact their deadly tolls in devastating earthquakes, droughts, and hurricanes—changes wrought by global warming and the depletion of fossil fuels threaten us today. "Now human beings live all over the globe, and the story always gets told by the victors," says Potts. "But we have to be careful with the narrative of our origins, because we, too, almost became extinct."

In an important but rarely remarked paradox, both of the dominant—and opposing—philosophical approaches to how best to dwell on our unpredictable earth conflict with the scientific record of our history here. It's clear that we live on a planet that's inherently unstable, says Potts, "so the biblical idea of dominion, which says that we control the world and can overcome all obstacles, just doesn't hold water." For the same reason, however, "neither does the so-called culture of preservation, which maintains that the earth had an original condition that we're destroying." Instead of hewing to these flawed theories, he says, "we need a new understanding of how we evolved in a changing world, so we can get it right in the future."

Our long up-and-down history of adapting to the shifts of our living planet is a moving testimony to the combination of *Homo novus*'s singularity and vulnerability. "Our existence on earth as one species is remarkable—a new mythic story," says Potts. "The many other branches and experiments in being human are no longer around, and we too had our endangered moment." There are tantalizing comparisons between the landmarks of our cultural evolution and scriptural lore, such as the exile from Eden/Africa for the pursuit of new, forbidden knowledge or catastrophic monsoons and Noah's flood. "I don't want to invoke the Bible, which stands as its own mythic story," says Potts, "but there are certain convergences."

According to Ecclesiastes, "The thing that hath been, it is that which shall be; and that which is done is that which shall be done: and there is no new thing under the sun." That dour writer never got to visit the Air and Space Museum, however, or play computer games with his cat.

## ACKNOWLEDGMENTS

First, I want to express my gratitude to Dr. C. Robert Cloninger for sharing some of his profound understanding of why we are the way we are and for reviewing my manuscript. His comments and corrections not only greatly improved this book but also amplified my own appreciation of neophilia.

I'm especially grateful to Richard Potts, David Zald, and Robert Kozinets for their insights and patience above and beyond the call of academic duty.

For their generosity in sharing their knowledge with me, I thank Steve Banks, Barbara Benedict, Kent Berridge, Roger Bohn, Esther Dyson, James Fowler, Seth Godin, Henry Harpending, James Higley, Michael Inzlicht, Laurent Itti, Jane Joseph, Jerome Kagan, Todd Kashdan, Arthur Kramer,

Donald Kraybill, Kate Stone Lucas, Grant McCracken, Viktor Mayer-Schönberger, Karen Mitchell, Story Musgrave, Clifford Nass, Daniel Pine, Daniel Pink, Simon Rich, Cheryl Rogowski, Mark Runco, Paul Saffo, Barry Schwartz, Paul Silvia, Dean Simonton, Patricia Spacks, Robert Sternberg, Stephen Suomi, Ian Tattersall, David Hurst Thomas, Robert Thompson, Oshin Vartanian, Robert Weisberg, Nathan Zeldes, and Marvin Zuckerman.

Finally, I thank Ann Godoff, my editor, who took on this book based on a single sentence and supplied the tough love it needed to grow. Ben Platt and the Penguin Press team were not only efficient but also models of mandarin courtesy. As always, I'm grateful to Kris Dahl, my agent, for her steadfast support.

# BIBLIOGRAPHY, SUGGESTED READINGS, AND NOTES

*The quoted material in this book comes from interviews conducted by the author, unless otherwise specified below. Readers who wish to pursue certain topics in more detail will also find representative publications by the individuals from many professions who have generously contributed their insights.*

## INTRODUCTION: WHAT'S NEW?

**5 In other words, they follow:** "Be not the first . . . " Alexander Pope, *Essay on Criticism* (1711) (London: British Library, Historical Print Editions, 2011).

**6 A word here about language:** Since their appearance in the late nineteenth century, *neophilia* and *neophobia* have meant different things in different contexts. To biologists, the terms simply refer to animals' tendency to be attracted to or avoid novelty. In *The Neophiliacs,* published in 1969, the English journalist and social critic Christopher Booker blamed novelty seekers for the social failings of the 1950s and 1960s. More recently, hackers, science-fiction buffs, futurists, and counterculture writers such as Robert Anton Wilson have touted *neophilia* as the sine qua non of modernity and progress.

## CHAPTER 1: HOW WE BECAME WHO WE ARE

**15 "America is now a space-faring nation":** "Aerospace: Mr. Mac and His Team," *Time,* March 31, 1967.

**16 Its exhibits, from touchable fossils:** Richard Potts and Christopher Sloan, *What Does It Mean to Be Human?* (Washington, DC: National Geographic Society, 2010).

**23 A paleoanthropologist at New York City's:** Ian Tattersall, *Paleontology: A Brief History of Life* (West Conshohocken, PA: Templeton, 2010).

**27 Their faces, so like yet unlike ours:** *John Dryden: The Major Works,* ed. Keith Walker (Oxford: Oxford University Press, 1987).

## CHAPTER 2: SURPRISE DETECTOR

**29 You have only to follow:** D. E. Berlyne, *Conflict, Arousal, and Curiosity* (New York: McGraw-Hill, 1960); D. E. Berlyne and W. J. Boudewijns, "Hedonic Effects of Uniformity in Variety," *Canadian Journal of Psychology* 25 (1971): 195–206; R. W. White, "Motivation Reconsidered: The Concept of Competence," *Psychological Review* 66 (1959): 297–333; E. L. Deci and R. M. Ryan, "Human Autonomy: The Basis for True Self-Esteem," *Efficacy, Agency, and Self-Esteem,* ed. M. Kemis (New York: Plenum, 1995).

**29 An inventive experiment offers:** Karen Mitchell, Marilyn Livosky, and Mara Mather, "The Weapon Focus Effect Revisited," *Legal and Criminological Psychology* 3 (1998): 287–303.

**30 The brain is conventionally portrayed:** L. Itti, P. F. Baldi, "Bayesian Surprise Attracts Human Attention," *Vision Research*, Vol. 49, No. 10 (May 2009): 1295–1306.

**30 To investigate what influences:** L. Itti, C. Koch, "Computational Modelling of Visual Attention," *Nature Reviews Neuroscience,* Vol. 2, No. 3 (March 2001): 194–203.

**32 In one such study:** R. A. Butler, "Curiosity in Monkeys," *Scientific American* (February 1954): 70–75.

**33 Arousal by and adaptation to:** Alan Slater, et al., "Orientation Discrimination and Cortical Function in the Human Newborn," *Perception* 17 (1988): 597–602.

**35 Merely introducing:** R. E. Clark and B. M. Sugrue, "Research on Instructional Media," *Educational Media Yearbook 1987–88*, ed. D. Ely (Littletown, CO: Libraries Unlimited, 1988).

**35 Underscoring the stimulating role:** Dean Simonton, *Genius 101* (New York: Springer, 2009).

**36 It's no accident:** Jonathan Shaw, "Leaves That Lunch," *Harvard Magazine* (May–June 2005).

**37 The late economist Tibor Scitovsky:** Tibor Scitovsky, *The Joyless Economy* (New York: Oxford, 1992).

**37 Encounters with a person:** M. Inzlicht, C. R. Kaiser, and B. Major, "The Face of Chauvinism: How Prejudice Expectations Shape Perceptions of Facial Affect," *Journal of Experimental Social Psychology* 44 (2008): 758–66.

**38 A hoarder stays aroused:** Randy Frost and Gail Steketee, *Stuff: Compulsive Hoarding and the Meaning of Things* (New York: Houghton Mifflin Harcourt, 2010).

**39 In June 2010, Erwin Evert:** Cory Hatch, "Griz Victim Knew of Trap," *Jackson Hole News & Guide*, June 23, 2010.

**39 One way to effect that:** Grant McCracken, *Culture and Consumption II: Markets, Meaning, and Brand Management* (Bloomington: Indiana University Press, 2005); Grant McCracken, *Chief Culture Officer: How to Create a Living, Breathing Corporation* (New York: Basic Books, 2009).

**41 He quotes the French geographer:** Fernand Braudel, *Capitalism and Material Life, 1400–1800* (New York: Harper and Row, 1973).

**41 When Ari Kiev:** William Grimes, "Ari Kiev, a Psychiatrist, Dies at 75," *New York Times,* November 30, 2009.

**CHAPTER 3: APPROACH, AVOID, OR MAYBE**

**45 The simplest is the brief:** To gauge surprise's intensity, neuroscientists Laurent Itti and Pierre Baldi propose a unit of measurement wonderfully called a *wow*, which you experience whenever a new observation changes your belief about or estimate of something by a factor of two. Thus, if you've heard on the radio that there's a 25 percent chance of rain today, but masses of dark clouds cause you to revise your estimate to a 50 percent chance, you've just registered one *wow* of surprise.

**45 A few moments of playing peekaboo:** Paul Silvia, *Exploring the Psychology of Interest* (New York: Oxford University Press, 2006); Paul Silvia, "Interest—The Curious Emotion," *Current Directions in Psychological Science* 17 (2008): 57–60; Paul Silvia, "Curiosity and Motivation," *Oxford Handbook of Motivation,* ed. R. M. Ryan (New York: Oxford University Press, 2011).

**46 The biographies of notably creative:** One morning in 1964, the famously hardworking Paul McCartney woke up with the melody for "Yesterday"— now history's most recorded song—playing in his head in such detail that he was convinced at first that it must be another composer's tune that he'd heard somewhere. Such breakthroughs seem utterly novel and sudden because the moment's intense arousal suppresses the memory of all of the previous heavy lifting.

**47 Speaking of innovative:** Albert Einstein, "On the Moral Obligation of the Scientist" (1952) *The Bulletin* (March 1979).

**50 Daniel Pink, a writer and lecturer:** Daniel Pink, *A Whole New Mind: Why Right Brainers Will Rule the Future* (New York: Riverhead, 2006).

**52 An interesting experiment on:** Roy Baumeister, et al., "Bad Is Stronger Than Good," *Review of General Psychology,* Vol. 5, No. 4 (2001): 323–70.

**52 Inzlicht and his students asked:** J. B. Hirsh and M. Inzlicht, "The Devil You Know: Neuroticism Predicts Neural Response to Uncertainty," *Psychological Science* 19 (2008): 962–67.

**54 In contrast to neophilic institutions':** Daniel Pink, *Drive: The Surprising Truth About What Motivates Us* (New York: Riverhead, 2009).

**56 All of us feel and function:** A. V. Kalueff and P. G. Zimbardo, "Behavioral Neuroscience, Exploration, and K. C. Montgomery's Legacy," *Brain Research Review* 53 (2007): 328–31.

**CHAPTER 4: YOU MEET NEW**

**59 For that matter, if you've:** David Sloan Wilson, *Evolution for Everyone: How Darwin's Theory Can Change the Way We Think About Our Lives* (New York: Delacorte Press, 2007).

**60 Even tiny infants express:** B. J. Roder, E. W. Bushnell, and A. M. Sasseville, "Infants' Preferences for Familiarity and Novelty During the Course of Visual Processing," *Infancy* 1 (2000): 491–507.

**60 Whether your own tendency:** Winifred Gallagher, *Just the Way You Are* (New York: Random House, 1996).

**64 The questionnaire-based "Big Five":** P. T. Costa and R. R. McCrae, *NEO Personality Inventory Professional Manual* (Odessa, FL: Psychological Assessment Resources, 1992).

**64 In one intriguing study:** S. B. Martin, et al., "The Human Right Anterior Hippocampus Is Larger in Experience-Seekers," *Neuropsychologia* 45 (2007): 2874–81.

**65 If people comment on your:** S. Gosling, *Snoop: What Your Stuff Says About You* (New York: Basic Books, 2008).

**65 First of all, the original:** C. G. DeYoung, et al., "Intellect as Distinct from Openness," *Journal of Personality and Social Psychology* 97 (2009): 883–92.

**66 According to Mark Runco:** Mark Runco, *Creativity: Theories and Themes* (Salt Lake City: Academic Press, 2006).

**66 As if explaining the Peter principle:** Robert Sternberg, *Wisdom, Intelligence, and Creativity Synthesized* (New York: Cambridge University Press, 2007).

**66 The legendary bongo-playing:** James Gleick, *Genius* (New York: Vintage, 1993).

**67 Finally, to the creative personality's:** C. Robert Cloninger, *Feeling Good: the Science of Well-Being* (New York: Oxford University Press, 2004).

**68 In his classic research:** Jerome Kagan, *The Temperamental Thread* (New York: Dana Foundation, 2010).

**68 Their physiological markers:** Jerome Kagan and Nancy Snidman, *The Long Shadow of Temperament* (Cambridge, MA: Harvard University Press, 2004); Carl Schwartz, et al., "Structural Differences in Adult Orbital and Ventromedial Prefrontal Cortex Predicted by Infant Temperament at 4 Months of Age," *Archives of General Psychiatry* 67 (2010): 78–84.

**71 In his primate populations:** Stephen Suomi, "Uptight and Laid-Back Monkeys: Individual Differences in Response to Social Challenges," *Plasticity of Development*, ed. S. Brauth, et al. (Cambridge, MA: MIT Press, 1991).

**72 As a child, Eleanor:** Joseph Lash, *Eleanor Roosevelt* (New York: Doubleday, 1964).

**74 Just as some temperament researchers:** W. F. McCourt, R. J. Gurrera, and H. S. Cutter, "Sensation Seeking and Novelty Seeking. Are They the Same?" *Journal of Nervous and Mental Disease* 5 (1993): 309–12.

**74 Lying in a dark, soundproofed:** Marvin Zuckerman, *Sensation Seeking and Risky Behavior* (Washington, DC: American Psychological Association, 2011); Marvin Zuckerman, *Behavioral Expressions and*

*Biosocial Bases of Sensation Seeking* (New York: Cambridge University Press, 1994).

**76 In 1996, Cloninger:** C. R. Cloninger, R. Adolfsson, and N. M. Svrakic, "Mapping Genes for Human Personality," *Nature Genetics* 12 (1996): 3–4; R. P. Ebstein, et al., "Dopamine D4 Receptor (D4DR) Exon III Polymorphism Associated with the Human Personality Trait of Novelty Seeking," *Nature Genetics* 12 (1996): 78–80.

**78 One study of eighty:** Inbal Kivenson Bar-On, "Fearlessness in Preschoolers: An Extreme End of the Approach and Withdrawal Temperamental Dimension," sponsored by the University of Haifa Faculty of Education, November 2010.

**79 In a complementary adult study:** F. M. Siem and M. W. Murray, "Personality Factors Affecting Pilot Combat Performance: A Preliminary Investigation," *Aviation Space Environmental Medicine* 65 (1994): 45–48.

## CHAPTER 5: THE ALCHEMY OF ANTICIPATION

**81 "Every day some new fact comes to light":** Elspeth Huxley, *Scott of the Antarctic* (London: Weidenfeld and Nicolson, 1977).

**82 Underscoring this connection:** J. W. Buckholtz, et al., "Dopaminergic Differences in Human Impulsivity," *Science* 329 (2010): 532; D. H. Zald, et al., "Midbrain Dopamine Receptor Availability Is Inversely Associated with Novelty-seeking Traits in Humans," *Journal of Neuroscience* 28 (2008): 14372–78.

**82 For a long time:** Morten L. Kringelbach and Kent C. Berridge, eds., *Pleasures of the Brain* (New York: Oxford University Press, 2009).

**84 The military already uses:** Daniel Gopher, et al., "Enhancing Flight Performance Through an Attentional Trainer Based on a Complex Computer Game" (technical report, Technion Research Center for Work Safety and Human Engineering, HEIS, May 1989).

**84 Duke University's behavioral economist:** Dan Ariely and George Loewenstein, "The Heat of the Moment," *Journal of Behavioral Decision Making*, 19 (2006): 87–98.

**86 Based on contemporaries' observations:** Edwin Legrand Sabin, *Kit Carson Days* (Memphis, TN: General Books LLC, 2010).

**86 To make a long, complicated story short:** The individuals who carry DRD4's 7R variant have fewer dopamine receptors, which also need much more of the transmitters than average in order to activate. The allele appears to have a number of effects in dopamine's target areas in the brain as well as on the firing properties of dopamine cells.

In addition to such "regular" receptors, which are located in the brain regions reached by the dopamine network, autoreceptors on the dopamine cells themselves also help control how much of the transmitter gets released. David Zald finds that neophiliacs have fewer autoreceptors for D2, and perhaps D3, than the average person. "Think of it this way," he says. "Dopamine would have the greatest impact in individuals who have a high number of postsynaptic receptors and a low number of autoreceptors, because that combination means that they won't control their dopamine balance as well. They'll release more of the transmitter, and it will be harder to regulate the level at the synapse."

**88 Robert Moyzis, a molecular geneticist:** James Swanson, et al., "Dopamine Genes and ADHD," *Neuroscience & Biobehavioral Review* 24 (2000): 21–25; Yuan-Chun Ding, et al., "Evidence of Positive Selection Acting at the Human Dopamine Receptor D4 Gene Locus," *Proceedings of the National Academy of Sciences* (January 2002); available at http://pnas.org/content/99/1/309.abstract—aff-1.

**91 Processing novelty involves an array:** This constellation of brain structures includes the ventral striatum, which mediates motivation and drive; the anterior cingulate cortex, which helps regulate inhibition and restraint; the nucleus accumbens, which is involved in handling rewards; the insula, which processes subjective emotion and visceral cravings; the basal ganglia, which aid in deciding what to do next; and the hippocampus, which helps you recognize, record, and recall new information.

**91 This touchy structure was long:** J. E. Joseph, et al., "fMRI in Alert, Behaving Monkeys: An Adaptation of the Human Infant Familiarization Novelty Preference Procedure," *Journal of Neuroscience Methods* 157 (2006): 10–24.

**91 Interestingly, the brains of neophiliacs:** J. E. Joseph, et al., "Neural Correlates of Emotional Reactivity in Sensation Seeking," *Psychological Science* 20 (2009): 215–23.

**92 Summarizing a lot of neuroscience:** In one experiment, Joseph asked some neophiles and neophobes to perform the deliberately boring task of looking at a series of images and flagging the unfamiliar ones among those they'd already seen. She figured that because they'd prefer to feel 100 percent confident that a picture was new, the cautious individuals would be likelier to say that an image was old than the bolder folks. To her surprise, however, the reverse was true. It seems that because they're naturally more risk-averse, neophobes are likelier to react to anything that might possibly be new because it could pose a threat.

Our different thresholds for responding to novelty are highlighted in an ingenious experiment in which neophiles and neophobes watched some jazzed-up public-service spots of the this-is-your-brain-on-drugs sort while their brains were scanned. Joseph was surprised to find that the especially exciting, fast-paced films activated the brain's novelty-sensitive structures in the cautious subjects but not in the bold. The neophobes' threshold for novelty is so low that even a little bit can activate the system and evoke a *Wow!* or an *Ugh!* In contrast, the neophiliacs' higher tolerance for arousal inclines them to think, "Gee, this video is lame. I need more excitement than this."

**93 Simplistic pop theories:** Oshin Vartanian, "Brain and Neuropsychology," *Encyclopedia of Creativity* (2nd ed.), eds. M. Runco and S. Pritzker,

(San Diego, CA: Academic Press, 2011); Oshin Vartanian, "Nature and Nurture," *Encyclopedia of Creativity*.

**97 Pine's study of teenage boys:** Daniel S. Pine, et al., "Anxiety and Anxiety Disorders in Children and Adolescents: Developmental Issues and Implications for DSM-V," *Anxiety Disorders*, Vol. 32, Iss. 3, (September 2009): 483–524; Daniel S. Pine, et al., "Amygdala and Ventrolateral Prefrontal Cortex Function During Anticipated Peer Evaluation in Pediatric Social Anxiety," *Archives of General Psychiatry*, Vol. 65, Iss. 11 (2008).

**98 An unsung nineteenth-century contemporary:** John Conway, "The Female Hunter of Long Eddy," *Sullivan County Democrat*, November 20, 2009.

CHAPTER 6: NOVELTY AND NURTURE

**103 Experiments with genetically fearful:** Stephen Suomi, "Uptight and Laid-Back Monkeys: Individual Differences in Response to Social Challenges," *Plasticity of Development*, ed. S. Brauth, et al. (Cambridge, MA: MIT Press, 1991).

**104 Where human beings are concerned:** Liisa Keltikangas-Järvinen, et al., "Nature and Nurture in Novelty Seeking," *Molecular Psychiatry* 9 (2004): 308–11.

**105 Research often focuses on:** Jaime E. Settle, et al., "Friendships Moderate an Association Between a Dopamine Gene Variant and Political Ideology," *Journal of Politics*, Vol. 72, No. 4, (2010): 1189–98.

**107 "My colleagues would have said":** S. L. Willis, et al., "Long-Term Effects of Cognitive Training on Everyday Functional Outcomes in Older Adults," *Journal of the American Medical Association* 296 (2006): 2805–14; Stanley Colcombe and Arthur F. Kramer, "Fitness Effects on the Cognitive Function of Older Adults: A Meta-Analytic Study," *Psychological Science*, Vol. 14, No. 2 (2001): 125–30; Charles H. Hillman, Kirk I. Erickson, and Arthur F. Kramer, "Be Smart, Exercise Your Heart," *Nature Reviews Neuroscience* 9 (2008): 58–65.

**111 Some provocative, underremarked research:** Bella Kotik-Friedgut, "Development of the Lurian Approach: A Cultural Neurolinguistic Perspective," *Neuropsychology Review*, Vol. 16, No. 1 (2006).

**112 Observing that Watson and Crick:** Robert Weisberg, "On 'Out-of-the-Box' Thinking in Creativity," *Tools for Innovation*, ed. A. Markman (New York: Oxford University Press, 2009).

**114 A study of a Kenyan tribe:** Dan T. A. Eisenberg, et al., "Dopamine Receptor Genetic Polymorphisms and Body Composition in Undernourished Pastoralists: An Exploration of Nutrition Indices Among Nomadic and Recently Settled Ariaal Men of Northern Kenya," *BMC Evolutionary Biology*, 8 (June 2008).

**115 Research conducted at the University:** Chuansheng Chen, et al., "Population Migration and the Variation of Dopamine D4 Receptor

(DRD4) Allele Frequencies Around the Globe," *Evolution and Human Behavior*, Vol. 20, No. 5 (1999): 309–24.

**116 At first, it's hard to believe:** Yuan-Chun Ding, et al., "Evidence of Positive Selection Acting at the Human Dopamine Receptor D4 Gene Locus," *Proceedings of the National Academy of Sciences*, Vol. 99, No. 1 (January 2002): 309–14; available at http://pnas.org/content/99/1/309.abstract—aff-1.

**116 University of Utah anthropologist:** Henry Harpending and Gregory Cochran, "In Our Genes," *Proceedings of the National Academy of Sciences*, Vol. 99, No. 1 (2002):10–12; Henry Harpending and Gregory Cochran, *The 10,000 Year Explosion: How Civilization Accelerated Human Evolution* (New York: Basic Books, 2010).

**117 In November 2010, the Chinese government:** Steve Lohr, "When Innovation, Too, Is Made in China," *New York Times*, January 2, 2011.

CHAPTER 7: CULTURE, CURIOSITY, AND BOREDOM

**122 Even the philosophical Greeks:** Roger Shattuck, *Forbidden Knowledge: From Prometheus to Pornography* (New York: St. Martin's Press, 1996).

**122 "The desire to search for something":** Barbara M. Benedict, *Curiosity: A Cultural History of Early Modern Inquiry* (Chicago: University of Chicago Press, 2001).

**127 A friend's offhand remark:** Patricia Meyer Spacks, *Boredom: The Literary History of a State of Mind* (Chicago: University of Chicago Press, 1995).

**129 Here is Martin Heidegger: "Profound boredom":** Martin Heidegger, *The Fundamental Concepts of Metaphysics* (Bloomington: Indiana University Press, 2001).

**130 In the twenty-first century, few would agree:** Oscar Wilde, *The Picture of Dorian Gray* (New York: Tribeca, 2011).

CHAPTER 8: THE EVER-NEW FRONTIER

**132 Indeed, Mark Twain complained:** Mark Twain, *Life on the Mississippi* (New York: Library of America, 2009).

**132 Summing up the national modus operandi:** Maira Kalman, *The Principles of Uncertainty* (New York: Penguin Press, 2007).

**133 When he's not seated:** David Hurst Thomas, "Engineering Alta Toquima: Social Investments and Dividends at 11,000 Feet," *Engineering Mountain Landscapes: An Archaeology of Social Investment*, eds. Maria N. Zedeño and Laura L. Scheiber (Salt Lake City: University of Utah Press, in press).

**140 Our passion for:** Robert Kozinets and Jay M. Handelman, "Adversaries of Consumption: Consumer Movements, Activism, and Ideology," *Journal of Consumer Research* 31 (2004): 691–704.

**140 One major reason for the:** Robert Kozinets, "Technology/Ideology: How Ideological Fields Influence Consumers' Technology Narratives," *Journal of Consumer Research* 34 (2008): 864–81.

**142 The strategy of "experience engineering":** B. Joseph Pine and James Gilmore, *The Experience Economy* (Boston: Harvard Business Press, 1999).

**143 The tacit cooperation between:** Douglas Atkin, *The Culting of Brands* (New York: Portfolio, 2004).

**144 "What moves those of genius, what inspires their work:** Hubert Wellington, *Journal of Delacroix* (New York: Phaidon Press, 1995).

**145 Even some enterprises:** Robert Kozinets, "Can Consumers Escape the Market? Emancipatory Illuminations from Burning Man," *Journal of Consumer Research* 29 (2002): 20–38.

**145 As Swarthmore psychologist Barry Schwartz:** Barry Schwartz, *The Paradox of Choice: Why More Is Less* (New York: Ecco Press, 2004); Barry Schwartz, "Self-Determination: The Tyranny of Freedom," *American Psychologist* 55 (2000): 79–88; Barry Schwartz, H. R. Markus, and A. C. Snibbe, "Is Freedom Just Another Word for Many Things to Buy?" *New York Times Magazine*, February 26, 2006.

CHAPTER 9: THE REALLY NEW AGE

**154 According to UC San Diego's:** available at http://hmi.ucsd.edu/howmuchinfo_research_report_consum.php.

**157 During 2009, forty-seven million:** National Endowment for the Arts, "How Technology Influences Arts Participation," June 2010; available at http://nea.gov/research/new-media-report/index.html.

**158 Research that MIT's innovation expert:** Eric von Hippel, et al., "Comparing Business and Household Sector Innovation in Consumer Products"; available at http://ssrn.com/abstract=1683503.

**159 Workplace savant Daniel Pink:** Daniel Pink, *A Whole New Mind: Why Right Brainers Will Rule the Future* (New York: Riverhead, 2006).

**160 Our smart tools also pull:** Robert Kozinets, et al., eds. "Social Media for Social Change," *Transformative Consumer Research to Benefit Global Welfare.* (In press.)

**161 Thus, USC media scholar:** Henry Jenkins, *Fans, Bloggers, and Gamers: Media Consumers in a Digital Age* (New York: NYU Press, 2006).

**162 In what some critics view:** Grant McCracken, *Chief Culture Officer: How to Create a Living, Breathing Corporation* (New York: Basic Books, 2009).

**164 "From one perspective":** Robert Kozinets, "Articulating the Meanings of Star Trek's Culture of Consumption," *Journal of Consumer Research* 28 (2001): 67–88.

**165 This unscripted form of entertainment:** Robert Thompson, *Television's Second Golden Age* (New York: Continuum, 1996).

**CHAPTER 10: NOVELTY MACHINES: FOR BETTER AND WORSE**

172 **First, some inventive psychologists:** Daniel Simons and Christopher Chabris, "Gorillas in Our Midst," *Perception* 28 (1999): 1059–74.

174 **A clever essay about:** Rand Richards Cooper, "It's My Party, and You Have to Answer," *New York Times*, March 14, 2010.

174 **Nevertheless, a *Wall Street Journal* poll:** "Taxi TVs Annoy Some, but Riders Can't Be Bothered with Off Switch," *Wall Street Journal*, April 27, 2010.

176 **As a father of young children:** Todd Kashdan, *Curious? Discover the Missing Ingredient to a Fulfilling Life* (New York: William Morrow, 2009).

178 **Citing that wise old maxim:** Viktor Mayer-Schönberger, *Delete: The Virtue of Forgetting in the Digital Age* (Princeton, NJ: Princeton University Press, 2009).

178 **Since 1998, Microsoft's venerable:** Gordon Bell and Jim Gemmell, *Total Recall: How the E-Memory Revolution Will Change Everything* (New York: Dutton, 2009).

183 ***Politico.com* has been described:** Jeremy Peters, "In a World of Online News, Burnout Starts Younger," *New York Times*, July 18, 2010.

**CHAPTER 11: CAUTION AHEAD: SILLY, UNFOCUSED, AND HOOKED?**

191 **"One thought in the mimetic community":** Seth Godin, *Poke the Box* (Amazon: Domino Project, 2011).

191 **In addition to the BP:** Yahoo.com, "2010 Year in Review: Top 10 Searches"; available at http://yearinreview.yahoo.com/2010/us_top_10 _searches#Top%2010%Searches.

193 **Nevertheless, as Maryanne Wolf:** "Curling Up with Hybrid Books, Videos Included," *New York Times*, September 30, 2009; Maryanne Wolf, *Proust and the Squid: The Story and Science of the Reading Brain* (New York: Harper Perennial, 2008).

193 **Technology's way of undermining:** Elisabeth Bumiller, "We Have Met the Enemy and He Is PowerPoint," *New York Times*, April 27, 2010.

196 **The basic mechanics of attention:** Winifred Gallagher, *Rapt: Attention and the Focused Life* (New York: Penguin Press, 2009).

197 **One study of sixteen- to eighteen-year-olds:** Larry Rosen, et al., "Multitasking Across Generations: Multitasking Choices and Difficulty Ratings in Three Generations of Americans," *Computers in Human Behavior*, Vol. 25, No. 2 (2009): 483–89.

197 **A large survey of media use:** Victoria J. Rideout, Ulla G. Foehr, and Donald F. Roberts, "Generation M 2: Media in the Lives of 8- to 18-Year-Olds," Kaiser Family Foundation Study; available at http://kff.org/entmedia/upload/8010.pdf, 2010.

197 **A study of four thousand teenagers:** Scott Frank, et al., "Hyper-texting and Hyper-networking: A New Health Risk Category for Teens?" *Proceedings of the American Public Health Association*, (November 2010).

**197 Research has shown that depressed people:** Lawrence T. Lam and Zi-Wen Peng, "Effect of Pathological Use of the Internet on Adolescent Mental Health: A Prospective Study," *Archives of Pediatrics and Adolescent Medicine*, Vol. 164, No. 10 (2010): 901–6.

**198 Nathan Zeldes, who's an IT engineer:** Nathan Zeldes, et al., "Infomania: Why We Can't Afford to Ignore It Any Longer," *First Monday*, Vol. 12, No. 8 (2007).

**198 The average knowledge worker:** Gloria Mark, et al., "No Task Left Behind? Examining the Nature of Fragmented Work," *Proceedings of the Association for Computing Machinery CHI*, Portland, OR (2005).

**199 In a famous experiment:** Ulric Neisser, *Cognition and Reality* (San Francisco: Freeman, 1976).

**200 (After navigating London's maze):** E. A. Maguire, et al., "Navigation-Related Structural Changes in the Hippocampi of Taxi Drivers," *Proceedings of the National Academy of Sciences* 97 (2000).

**200 In fact, research conducted:** Eyal Ophir, Clifford Nass, and Anthony D. Wagner, "Cognitive Control in Media Multitaskers," *Proceedings of the National Academy of Sciences*, Vol. 106, No. 33 (2009): 15583–87.

**202 (A large study of Parkinson's):** Mark Stacy, et al., "Pathological Gambling Associated with Dopamine Agonist Therapy in Parkinson's Disease," *Neurology* 61 (2003): 422–23.

**203 After her first bad accident:** Robert Siegel, *All Things Considered*, September 23, 2009.

CHAPTER 12: NAVIGATING WITH NEOPHILIA

**210 "If I ask you":** M. F. Steger, et al., "Understanding the Search for Meaning in Life: Personality, Cognitive Style, and the Dynamic Between Seeking and Experiencing Meaning," *Journal of Personality* 76 (2008): 199–228; T. B. Kashdan, et al., "The Curiosity and Exploration Inventory-II," *Journal of Research in Personality* 43 (2009): 987–98; T. B. Kashdan and J. Rottenberg, "Psychological Flexibility as a Fundamental Aspect of Health," *Clinical Psychology Review* 30 (2010): 865–78; Todd B. Kashdan and Paul J. Silvia, "Curiosity and Interest: The Benefits of Thriving on Novelty and Challenge," *Handbook of Positive Psychology*, eds. C. R. Snyder and S. J. Lopez (New York: Oxford University Press, 2009).

**211 For the same reason:** Debra Mashek and Arthur Aron, eds., *Handbook of Closeness and Intimacy* (London: Psychology Press, 2004).

**211 One of the most surprising findings:** Mihaly Csikszentmihalyi, *Flow: The Psychology of Optimal Experience* (New York: Harper, 1991).

**211 As William James tells us:** William James, "Attention," in *The Principles of Psychology* (Cambridge, MA: Harvard University Press, 1981), chapt. 11.

**214 "It's more likely that":** Simon Rich, *Elliot Allagash* (New York: Random House, 2010).

**219 In a classic older study:** Ithiel De Sola Pool, Hiroshi Inose, and N. Takasaki, *Communication Flows: A Census in the United States and Japan* (New York: Elsevier, 1984).

**223 "Their basic question is":** D. B. Kraybill, *The Riddle of Amish Culture* (Baltimore, MD: Johns Hopkins University Press, 2001); D. B. Kraybill and C. Bowman, *On the Backroad to Heaven: Old Order Hutterites, Mennonites, Amish, and Brethren* (Baltimore, MD: Johns Hopkins University Press, 2001).

**229 "Be regular and orderly in your life like a bourgeois:** Gustave Flaubert, Francis Steegmuller, *The Letters of Gustave Flaubert* (Cambridge, MA: Harvard University Press, 1980).

# INDEX